REST STOPS

for

SINGLE MOTHERS

REST STOPS

f o r

INGLE OTHERS

Devotions To Encourage
You On Your Journey

Susan Titus Osborn & Lucille Moses

BROADMAN
& HOLMAN
PUBLISHERS

Nashville, Tennessee

© 1995 by Susan Titus Osborn & Lucille Moses

Published by
Broadman & Holman Publishers, Nashville, Tennessee

Design: Steven Boyd

Printed in the United States of America

4253-85
0-8054-5385-7

Dewey Decimal Classification: 242.643
Subject Heading: Devotional Literature \ Women—Religious Life
Library of Congress Card Catalog Number: 94-36905

Unless otherwise indicated, Scripture quotations are taken from the Holy Bible, New International Version, copyright © 1973, 1978, 1984 by International Bible Society. Verses marked LAB are from the NIV Life Application Bible, © 1991, Tyndale House (Wheaton, Ill.) and Zondervan; NASB, New American Standard Bible, © the Lockman Foundation, 1960, 1962, 1963, 1968, 1971, 1972, 1973, 1975, 1977; used by permission; RSV, Revised Standard Version of the Bible, copyrighted 1946, 1952, © 1971, 1973; and TLB, The Living Bible, copyright © Tyndale House Publishers, Wheaton, Ill., 1971, used by permission.

Other quotations are from *Bartlett's*; Biola University Employee Bulletin 4:18; *List of Quotations*; *Decision* magazine, "Reflections" and article on John Bunyan; Association of Handicapped Artists' Calendar; Salesian Missions' booklet, "Another Day," 2; *Christian Herald*, "Patchwork"; Discipleship Journal (1986) 32:25.

Library of Congress Cataloging-in-Publication Data
Osborn, Susan Titus, 1944–
Rest stops for single mothers: devotions to encourage you on your journey/ Susan Titus Osborn, Lucille Moses.
    p. cm.
  ISBN 0-8054-5385-7
  1. Single mothers—Prayer-books and devotions—English. 2. Single parents—Prayer-books and devotions—English. I. Moses, Lucille, 1929– . II. Title.
BV4596.S48082 1995
242'.6431—dc20
94-36905
CIP

Contents

Foreword

I have been privileged to minister to many individuals, but the one who reaches deeply into my heart is the single mom. I, myself, grew up in a single parent home. My mom and dad divorced when I was two months old. I didn't meet my dad until I was sixteen. Mom raised three of us boys alone, and she made each one of us feel special. I wish books such as *Rest Stops for Single Mothers: Devotions to Encourage You on Your Journey* would have been available for my mom.

Susan Titus Osborn and Lucille Moses have written a series of devotionals to encourage the growing number of single mothers who represent nearly half of our nation's families today. Both authors have lived as single mothers, so their knowledge of this issue is from their own personal experiences.

This book provides inspiration to help single moms cope with their situations, face their issues, and experience victory in their lives.

Dr. John Trent
President
Encouraging Words

Introduction

A caterpillar imprisons itself for a time in a cocoon. To survive and fulfill its function in life, the caterpillar must struggle and fight its way out of that prison. Upon emerging into the sunlight, it spreads its beautiful, butterfly wings in colorful splendor as it reflects the glory of God, its Creator.

New beginnings are never easy, especially when traumatic events are thrust upon us. If your home was broken up, by death or divorce, grief at first consumed you. Anger and resentment may have caused you to ask, "Why did this happen?"

You tried to be an understanding and loving spouse. Now, torn apart in a divorce court, dividing up your children and your life's possessions with someone who now seems like a stranger, you ask, "Why did life deal me such a blow?"

Perhaps you have always been a single parent and have shouldered the total responsibility of raising your children. Possibly your mate suffered an accident or became ill, and death crept into the scene. Now you are alone.

Whatever your situation, life as a single parent can be cold and empty. You have no one with whom to share your joys and sorrows. Even your children cannot fill the gaping hole left in your heart. Can you identify with these feelings? Many women defend against the possibility of further pain by weaving a cocoon of emotional isolation around themselves.

However, life will not stand still waiting for you to recover. What better time is there than now to pick up the pieces and take stock of what remains? Now is the time to decide what kind of person you want to see emerge from the brokenness.

A new beginning is never easy. At times, you may want to slip back into grief and anger. If that happens, allow God to guide you in setting new goals and finding new friends. This will bring some stability back into your life, as well as your children's lives.

Trials and testings are inevitable. Sometimes it will be hard to think and act sensibly, but do not give up. Eventually, healing will begin.

The apostle Paul wrote to Titus, his young friend and helper, with excellent advice we can use today. Paul reminded Titus that God instructs us to be sensible and of sound mind. We are to be examples to others.

Choices need to be made every day—many choices. If we face these one at a time with wisdom and a positive attitude, we will become a guiding influence and example to our children, our families, and others.

Jesus, our Lord, also faced rejection and loneliness. We have the resources of His enabling power to encourage and lift up others, even through our own pain and sorrow. Let's put Paul's instructions into practice.

Like the caterpillar, we also must struggle to break out of our cocoons—the protective covering we have woven around ourselves. We, too, can emerge to bask in the sunlight of God's love and ultimately reflect the glory and beauty which He had in mind when He created us.

A new beginning? Yes, indeed. The time is now.

✳

New Beginnings

CHAPTER ONE

Losing a loved one is hard, whether by death or divorce. When our lives become fractured, we are no longer whole. Depression sets in, especially when we are compelled to make one of the most difficult decisions of our lives—the divorce decision. In our grief, we bargain with God. Denial, anger, and bitterness become evident. However, we can overcome our disappointments and break through their confining barriers. We can do this by developing a close relationship with Jesus Christ and by depending on Him for our strength. He will enable us to let go of the past and willfully start a new beginning.

*

Perfect Shells and Broken Pieces

Adverse circumstances can usher us into the awesome
presence of a God we've served for many years,
and yet have never known.
AUTHOR UNKNOWN

I walked along the beach one autumn morning, hoping to find shells for my collection. The summer tourists had gone home, and the kids had returned to school. The beach was deserted except for an elderly couple walking hand in hand and a man scavenging with a metal detector. I seemed to be the only person searching for shells.

However, all I could find were broken pieces. I kicked at the sand in frustration. The broken shells reminded me of the fragmented pieces of my own life since the breakup of my marriage.

The wind whipped my hair and sent a chill down my back. I pulled my sweatshirt around me and kept walking. Somehow, I hoped my brisk pace would help me leave my problems behind to be swept out with the tide. Instead, the waves kept bringing in more and more broken shells.

Then, I paused and cried out, "Where are You, Lord? What plan do You have for the broken pieces of my life?"

I resumed walking, trying to gain some perspective on my situation. What had happened to my perfect little family of four? Like the shells, my hopes and dreams for the future had been dashed on the rocks.

God seemed silent. Yet, I sensed the fault was mine, not His. I wasn't seeking His guidance so much as I was venting my anger by shouting.

Another wave surged on the shore, and I continued my search. To my surprise, this one brought in a beautiful whole shell. Scooping it up in my hand, I turned it over and noticed how perfectly God had formed it. In the midst of all this brokenness was wholeness.

Perhaps God would make me whole, too. However, I needed to do my part. Instead of dwelling on my problems and unmet expectations, I needed to plan for the future. I no longer had a husband, but I did have two wonderful teenage boys. The three of us were still a family.

We could build on what we did have. We could love and encourage each other. We could laugh and plan inexpensive outings together. We could look to the future, knowing God would guide our path if we allowed Him.

Perhaps, if I stopped shouting at God, I would be able to hear Him speak. I looked at the perfect shell in my hand and smiled. Had God already spoken? — S.T.O.

"Cast all your anxiety on him because he cares for you."
1 PETER 5:7

Dear God,
please take the broken fragments of my life and make me
whole. Help me not to dwell on the past but to look to the
future, armed with Your presence. Amen.

✳

Out of the Depth

We are healed of a suffering
only by experiencing it to the full.
MARCEL PROUST

Nancy heaved a sigh of relief and said, "I'm so thankful God pulled me out of that depression. It plagued me for years. It took awhile, but He has worked in my life in amazing ways." She sat pensively looking into the distance and remembering.

To look at her it is difficult to believe she has gone through years of depression. She is a lovely woman.

"What caused your depression?" I asked.

She drew her thoughts back to the present and answered, "My marriage was not happy. My husband was an alcoholic. I didn't realize that he needed help when we were married."

"Did you go for counseling?" I asked.

"We both went to counseling for awhile, at my insistance." Nancy continued, "He put on such a good act that he was able to fool everyone. He never admitted he had a problem, so the counseling didn't help."

"How did that make you feel?"

"I became angry and resentful. I didn't want to be near him when he was drinking. The continual pain of living with an alcoholic made big changes in my life."

"When did your depression begin?" I asked.

"When my daughter was three. Negative feelings built up inside me, but I kept stuffing them down. I became more and more depressed. I had taken all I could handle without exploding. I just couldn't live that way anymore."

"What did you do then?" I questioned.

"I told him we were going to be a family together or not at all. He hadn't been coming home after work until late. He took no responsibility toward our family. His heart was not in our marriage. That really hurt."

"It's painful when someone you love and trust seems to care so little," I said.

"I tried to keep our marriage together," Nancy continued. "I wanted a loving relationship, but he didn't. I did everything I knew to do, with no results, so I gave up. I had given and given until I had nothing left to give. He refused to provide anything in return, so my desire for a relationship died. Finally, I asked him to leave."

"Did you seek counseling for yourself?" I asked.

"Yes, I had a good therapist. Also, my mother encouraged me to go to Alanon. That helped me put my life back together. I did a great deal of reading to understand alcoholism and a lot of praying. God was there for me.

"After our divorce, it took four or five years before I sensed significant recovery and found my real self again. At last, I'm out from under that burden. I thank God every day." Her face glowed with enthusiasm.

Sometimes it's necessary to prayerfully seek professional help when we have done everything we know to do. Through God's guidance, He can comfort and heal us through those who are trained to assist us. — L.M.

"Come to Me, all you who are weary and burdened, and I will give you rest."
MATTHEW 11:28

Father,
how we need Your touch when depression fills us with fear,
dragging us down and paralyzing us. Pull us out of its depths
and into Your healing grace. Amen.

✳

Divorce: The Only Alternative

It takes two to get married but only one to get a divorce.
AUTHOR UNKNOWN

Rich has been in a car accident. His head broke the windshield, and his neck is injured." My voice sounded on the edge of hysteria as I phoned my husband late one afternoon in 1986.

"Rich drove home after the accident, but I'm afraid to drive him to the hospital with the windshield shattered. Can you come home and take us?"

"No, I'm in a business meeting," was the curt reply on the other end of the telephone line.

At the hospital later that day, I had time to think while Rich went through a series of tests and x-rays. While I sat in the stillness of the waiting room, my husband's reaction to Rich's accident played over in my mind.

It made me realize what an enormous chasm had opened up between my husband of over twenty years and myself. He had quit attending church and no longer took part in most of our family activities.

During that difficult time, I went out of my way to do special things for him. However, the more I tried, the worse the situation became. He reacted by lashing out. Nothing seemed to please him, and he became more distant. He found excuses to go on prolonged business trips. In time, he was gone more than he was home—at night and on weekends.

I now realize God used Rich's accident to open my eyes to my husband's growing indifference. Even so, I prayed for God's guidance for almost a year before making the divorce decision. My health was failing, and my wise family doctor said, "I want you to obtain a six-month legal separation from your husband. Then you can better determine whether or not you can work things out."

Looking back, I feel that my greatest error was allowing this situation to drag on. Shortly after my husband and I separated, I realized that he had already forsaken the relationship. It could not be restored, and divorce was the only alternative.

Several years later when I asked my sons if they felt any regrets regarding the divorce, they both replied, "You should have made the decision years earlier and not put us through all the tension."

However, I had to be sure. It isn't easy to throw away a twenty-two-year marriage. I needed to reach a point, through prayer and counseling, where I realized divorce was unavoidable.

Today, I realize my ex-husband had abandoned both God and his family. God knew he would not change, and God does not interfere with an individual's free will. I am totally at peace regarding my decision, which I feel was completely within God's will. — S.T.O.

"But if the unbeliever leaves, let him do so. A believing man or woman is not bound in such circumstances; God has called us to live in peace."
1 CORINTHIANS 7:15

Dear God,
sometimes what is in Your plan for us is better than what we
ask. Thank You for helping us with decisions even before we
are ready to make them ourselves. Amen.

✳

"No, God!"

Necessity never made a good bargain.
BENJAMIN FRANKLIN

No, God! Please! Don't take my husband. I can't survive without him. Please let him live. I'll do anything You want." Jessica raised a tear-stained face to the ceiling. She ran her fingers across her swollen eyelids and brushed her hair back from her forehead.

As she tried to stand, she clung to the side of the bed for support. Her legs were weak from kneeling beside her husband's bed. The home care nurse entered the room. "Jessica, you need to rest. Why don't you lie down?"

Jessica gazed glassy-eyed at the nurse. She finally nodded her head and wandered off to fall across her bed in the next room. However, she couldn't sleep. Her husband of thirty-one years lay dying. She knew it was beyond her control, but she still tried to bargain for his life.

"Oh, God, You can't be so cruel as to take Jerry from me. How could I go on? I'll do anything. Anything! Tell me what to do, and I'll do it. I'll give You whatever You want. Just tell me. Anything, God, anything!"

Without warning, her husband had become seriously ill. The doctor said there was a good chance he would not recover. Jessica's world had been so orderly and controlled, and now it seemed to spin crazily out of control.

As the days went by, Jerry grew weaker and weaker. The doctor talked seriously with Jessica, trying to prepare her for the inevitable. Even so, she continued to plead with God for her husband's life.

A few days later, Jerry opened his eyes and looked at her. She took his hand in hers and kissed it. He smiled a weak smile, and then he looked beyond her as though he was viewing a different scene.

"It's beautiful, my dear," he whispered. He glanced at Jessica one more time and closed his eyes. He was gone.

Jessica stared at the body lying on the bed, and knew her husband was no longer there. Finally, utterly spent, she slumped over his body and her tears soaked the bed.

The doctor offered her a sedative when he arrived, but she refused it. "My husband's last words will sustain me.

"He went with such peace in his heart," she said wistfully. "I wish I had been able to see what he saw."

The next time Jessica saw the doctor, she said, "I tried to bargain with God for Jerry's life. That was selfish of me, because it was praying for my will to be done. Now I realize that instead of pleading with Him, I should have placed my confidence in His wisdom and love, knowing that He carries out the plan He has for each of our lives—mine as well as Jerry's."

Jessica sold their home and moved into a small apartment. She is slowly, but bravely, coming to terms with her new life. Many friends have reached out to love and comfort her. As she lives her life, one day at a time, her confidence in God's loving care sustains her. — L.M.

"Precious in the sight of the Lord
is the death of his saints."
PSALM 116:15

Father God,
thank You for not always granting our pleading with our
desired results. The wise and loving plans of Your heart are
always for our best. We praise You. Amen.

*

"I'm Fine. I'm Fine!"

Those who walk with God always get to their destination.
AUTHOR UNKNOWN

When I was going through my divorce, people often asked me, "How are you doing?"

I'd always reply, "I'm fine. I'm fine." It wasn't that I was trying to hide my feelings. I just felt so much better than I had for the three-year period that preceded my divorce decision that I responded, "I'm fine," even though I wasn't.

During the last few years of my marriage, my husband traveled most of the time. When he was home, we rarely did social things together. I developed my own friendships, my own social life, and my own church activities.

Even after he moved out of the house, my life changed little. My work, my friends, my church all remained the same. Unconsciously, I could pretend that nothing had changed. It was easy for me to live in denial.

My best friend, Lucille, kept asking me to join her at her church singles' group. Time after time, I turned her down. Finally one day, she said, "I wish you'd come Tuesday night. I'm teaching a class on forgiveness, and I know you could use a little help in that area."

I realized Lucille was right. I was angry at my ex-husband for hurting me and our sons. Plus, I hadn't begun to forgive him. After much prodding, I agreed to go.

Normally, I am outgoing, and I take crowds and new adventures in stride. However, this Tuesday night's outing was different. Driving the short distance to Lucille's church, my heart pounded. My palms were sweaty on the steering wheel. I felt as if I were wearing a big "D" for "divorced" on my blouse. One of the most difficult things I have ever done was walking through the double doors of the Single Parent Fellowship of the First Evangelical Free Church of Fullerton that night. It was my first big step toward admitting I was single. It took several meetings before I was comfortable entering those double doors. Yet, in time, that group became my second family.

My sons and my extended family were very supportive of my divorce decision, but they had their own lives to live. I needed to develop friendships with those who had been through similar experiences. I continued to attend the support group, and I continued to heal. Every time someone asked me how I was, I'd reply, "I'm fine."

Whenever Lucille heard me say, "I'm fine," she'd tell me, "You're 'finer' than you were the last time someone asked," and we would laugh. It became a joke between us.

Thanks to Lucille and many others, today I do feel fine. Plus, I realize that healing is a process. The journey back to wholeness takes a long time, but God stands beside us every step of the way.

Today when people ask me how I am, I still say, "I'm fine." Then I look at Lucille, and she just smiles. — S.T.O.

"The Lord will watch over your coming and going both now and forevermore."
PSALM 121:8

Dear God,
help us to invite You to accompany us on our journey back to
wholeness. We thank You for supportive friends who make
that journey easier. Amen.

*

Dispel the Anger

Anger is one of the sinews of the soul; he that wants it hath a
maimed mind.
THOMAS FULLER

The ringing of my phone pierced the quiet night. My friend Sally wailed, "Paul has left us. Can you come over?"

She flung herself into my arms, weeping. After holding her, I gently led her to the sofa.

"What happened?" I asked.

"It was terrible. After the children left for school, Paul said, 'Sally, I want a divorce. I don't love you anymore.'" She could barely utter the painful words.

"That doesn't sound like Paul," I said.

"I couldn't believe it," Sally cried out. "I am still in shock! He didn't think I loved *him* anymore, that I had no time for him. I told him that wasn't true, but he wouldn't listen." Tears poured down her grief-stricken face.

"Is there more?"

"Yeesss!" she moaned. "He has found someone else." Sally put her head in her hands. Her body shook as she sobbed out her anguish. "How can I tell the children?"

Sally and Paul had been married fifteen years. They had two lovely children—ten-year-old Tommy and eight-year-old Marilee. Sally was an attractive woman, but the swollen face I now saw in front of me was not pretty.

Sally struggled through the following days. As the weeks passed, I noticed a change. Her shock and disbelief turned to anger. Bitterness followed. She belittled Paul at every opportunity, particularly to the children.

Paul was entitled to the children every other weekend. When they came home, Sally grilled them for every minute detail—what their father had said, what they had done, who they had seen. Along with the bitterness, she became obsessed with a need for revenge.

After watching her behavior fluctuations for several months, I asked her if we could talk. She had changed so much. It was an embittered, angry woman that answered the door.

When we sat down, I said, "Sally, you're a dear friend. I'm worried that you're letting this situation with Paul drain you. Tommy and Marilee love you both, but they're afraid to talk to you about their daddy. They're hurting. You *must* get some help. You can't continue like this."

It was a long time before Sally could look objectively at the divorce. She eventually came to realize she was injuring not only herself, but also her children. She did not want to admit that her inattention to Paul had played a major part in their separation. However, finally she did.

Sally still has a long way to go to totally release her anger and bitterness, but she is trying, with God's help. Her children are not afraid anymore. She has stopped belittling their father.

Anger can be positive, but bitterness never is. It is easy, when our world is torn apart, to allow anger to creep in. It's what we *do* with that anger that matters. Sometimes we need to step back from a situation and view it objectively. Anger can destroy more than we realize.

My friend Sally can attest to that. But now, her face once again shows its loveliness, and recently I even heard her laugh. — L.M.

"Cease from anger, and forsake wrath;
Fret not yourself, it leads only to evildoing."
PSALM 37:8 NASB

Dear God,
help us to be willing to release our anger and bitterness, even
when we are deeply wounded. Instead, teach us to rest in
Your great love. Amen.

✻

The Next Five Minutes

If faith can be seen every step of the way, it is not faith.
WILLIAM BARCLAY

As I glanced around the grocery store, an uneasy feeling came over me. I felt like I was going to burst into tears. Since I had only one item in my grocery cart, I put it back on the shelf, rushed out of the store, and drove home.

In the solitude of my living room I prayed, "Lord, when will it end? When will I feel normal again? Why can't I even do my grocery shopping without bursting into tears?" I wanted instant answers to my years of problems. I didn't want to wait for God's timing.

The next weekend, my oldest son came home from college and took me out to lunch. Afterwards, we went shopping at the mall. All of a sudden, that overwhelming feeling I had experienced in the grocery store came over me again. I sat down on a bench in the center of the mall and burst into tears.

Rich sat down beside me and placed his arm around my shoulder. "Don't cry, Mom. I know it's hard."

"I'm sorry, Rich. I don't mean to embarrass you. Whenever I'm in a crowd, I experience this overwhelming feeling. It's so silly to cry, but I just can't help it."

"Mom, you were married to Dad over twenty years. You can't expect to get over him in a week. Allow yourself some time."

Through my tears, I smiled at the wise words of my firstborn son. "Go and finish your shopping. I'll wait here," I suggested.

"Are you sure you'll be OK?" Rich stared at me with genuine concern wrinkling his forehead.

"Yes. I have to conquer this fear of crowds, or I'll never be able to get on with my life."

Rich headed down the mall, and I leaned back on the bench. While I rested, I said a silent prayer, "Lord, get me through the next five minutes. Sustain me until my son returns."

Soon Rich returned with several packages in tow. His face lit up. "I found everything I needed, Mom. Thanks for waiting. You look much better."

"I prayed that God would get me through the next five minutes."

"He did," Rich said with confirmation.

I frowned. "Yes, but how will I get through tomorrow, next week, next year? I feel so overwhelmed being single again at my age. Plus, I'm worried about how you and Mike are going to make it through college."

Rich sat down next to me on the bench and took my hand. "You just answered your own question, Mom. Always pray that God will get you through the next five minutes, and He will."

God doesn't promise us strength for next week or next year, but He always promises us strength for today. That is all that matters.

That day I knew I would no longer suffer from a problem with crowds, and I haven't. God has always sustained me through the next five minutes. — S.T.O.

"Look at the birds of the air; they do not sow or reap or store away in barns, and yet your heavenly Father feeds them. Are you not much more valuable than they?"
MATTHEW 6:26

Dear Lord,
help us not to worry about the future. Teach us to depend on
You for our strength daily. Thank You for getting us through
each day. In Jesus' name, Amen.

✳

Letting the Stuffing Out

Wonderful things can happen to us when we live expectantly,
believe confidently, and pray affirmatively.
WILLIAM WARD

Have you ever come home and found your clothes, along with your daughter's, packed and sitting on the floor?" Ellen asked.

"You're joking?" I exclaimed.

"No, I'm not," Ellen answered. "I came home from work and found a woman sitting with John, my husband. He said, 'Ellen, this woman is from Van Lines. She is going to move you out.'"

"Why?" I asked in unbelief.

"When he found out I was pregnant with our second child, he became angry. He didn't want another child."

"Where did you go?"

"Back to my folks in California. It meant crossing the United States since we lived in Florida. My parents were exceptionally generous. All they asked was help with groceries, so I sold cosmetics."

"Did John care when the baby was born?" I asked.

"Actually, he never saw her. He was killed in a helicopter accident before she was born," Ellen responded.

"How horrible!"

"Yes, it was. I was concerned about him primarily because I had been praying for him to accept Jesus as his Savior and Lord, but he hadn't done that yet. Later, some of his friends told me John had phoned them the night before the accident and said he had made a terrible mistake."

"About you?" I asked.

"He didn't say. Later, I learned he also met with the pastor on the day before the accident. The pastor told him about Jesus and salvation, but John wasn't receptive. At least he was truthful.

"I may be wrong, but I feel God used the accident to get John's attention. He didn't die instantly, from what I was told. He had several minutes to think. I hope he reached out to the Lord."

"How did you handle that?"

"I stuffed everything inside of me—for about ten years! I refused to deal with it. Later, I began attending church. Pastor Charles Swindoll gave a series on grace—I cried through every sermon. It was healing to hear about God's grace and to realize He genuinely loved me. Finally, I began to let my feelings come out."

"How did your girls get along without a father, even though they had their grandfather?" I asked.

"They had a hard time because I had never coped with John's death while they were young. We're dealing with it now in therapy and undoing years of wrong because I was so resistant. My youngest daughter is angry because she never knew him. My oldest girl still struggles with nightmares about death. I feel responsible for their problems. I should have been open and honest with them."

Ellen smiled a hopeful smile and said, "All I can do now is pray and trust God to break down barriers and open up channels of communication between us. I know He will work everything out. Things are already looking up, and I'm thankful for that."

There are times in our lives when all we can do is let go, reach out in prayer to God, and trust Him to answer the needs of our hearts. — L.M.

"Then you will call upon Me and come and pray to Me,
and I will listen to you."
JEREMIAH 29:12, NASB

*Hear our prayers, Oh Lord, and bring Your balm to soothe
and console our needs. Remind us that You listen intently
when we pray to You. In Jesus' name, Amen.*

✻

Looking at Ourselves

CHAPTER TWO

Often, living through difficult circumstances, we lose our identity. Our self esteem is badly damaged. Understanding what has happened is easier if we can take a good look at ourselves and evaluate our circumstances. Who are we? Does a failed marriage mean that we are failures? We're vulnerable, and loneliness invades us. Our hearts cry out for acceptance of ourselves and God's love. We seek fulfillment.

✳

Making Others Miserable

Time and prayer are two important ingredients in the healing process, along with a real desire to go on . . . and not wallow in the misery.

<small>ANDREA WELLS MILLER</small>

How many times do I have to ask you to take out the trash? Can't you do anything without my having to tell you over and over?" Frances yelled at Ryan, her sixteen-year-old son.

"I'll take it out. Don't blow a gasket, Mom!" Ryan replied. As he passed his sister in the hallway, he whispered, "Be careful."

"Nancy, you get in here and do these dishes!" Frances's shrill voice rang out from the kitchen.

"I'm coming," Nancy replied.

Frances stomped upstairs. Larry, Nancy's younger brother, stood beside her at the sink. "What's gotten into Mom lately? We can't do anything to please her."

"I know," Nancy said. "I guess she's upset because of the divorce. We have to try to get along with her."

Ryan came inside and joined them. "I wish we could talk to Mom, but she flies off the handle at every little thing."

"Oh, I do, do I?" came an angry voice from the hallway.

"Mom!" Nancy exclaimed in exasperation. "We know you're unhappy about Dad being gone, but you shouldn't take it out on us. We love you, but what you're doing hurts."

Frances stared at her children for a few moments. Tears filled her eyes. "I guess you're right," she said. "I'm so hurt over your father leaving, I can't seem to get control of myself. I've had to assume all his responsibilities. With that and the demands of my job, I guess I've taken out my frustrations on you."

"Yes—and you're making our lives miserable. You never say a word about the good things we do. You're not being fair," Ryan said angrily. He paused, and in a softer tone he said, "We love you, Mom, but you make us feel like you don't want us anymore. Should we go live with Dad? He'd be glad to have us."

Frances sank into a chair by the table. "No! I want you to stay here. What a mess I've made of things. I'm sorry. I've been impatient with you—selfish and unbearable. I haven't thought about your feelings, because I've felt like a failure."

"You're not a failure with us, Mama," Larry spoke timidly.

Frances looked carefully at each face. "You know I love all of you, don't you?"

They nodded in unison.

"Mom," Nancy said softly, "God wants us to live together in love. He says so in His Word."

Frances, eyes glistening, looked at her precious teens. She opened her arms wide. "Maybe we can start over again. What do you say?"

They huddled around Frances. Their arms encircled her and each other. Changes would be made in their lives—that very day. — L.M.

"I urge you to live a life worthy of the calling you have received. Be completely humble and gentle; be patient, bearing with one another in love."

EPHESIANS 4:1–2

Father God,
help me to be honest about those qualities which do not honor
You. Instill in me the desire to become more patient and
loving. Amen.

*

Weather Vane or Crossbow

My life is my message.

MAHATMA GANDHI

A weather vane or a crossbow—which one describes
you?" challenged Wightman Weese, a Tyndale editor who
spoke at a seminar I was attending. He continued, "Both
have arrows, both point in any direction. The difference
is their source of power, and that source determines their
effectiveness."

A picture formed in my mind of the rooster weather
vane on top of my aunt's house. Whichever way the wind
blew, the rooster pointed in that direction. The weather
vane reacted to the forces acting upon it.

I remembered visiting my aunt during the last years
of my marriage. I watched that old copper rooster spin-
ning around, and I identified with it. I felt as if I were
tossing and turning in the wind, reacting to my husband's
whims.

One moment he might say, "Why don't you stay home
more often? The children need you." I'd cancel some of
my activities, but find myself bored at home since my boys
were either at school or at swim team practice. After a little
cleaning, there wasn't much for me to do alone at home.

The next time I'd have a conversation with him, he'd
comment, "Don't you have any social life? How come you

27

sit home all the time?" So I'd resume my volunteer work and church activities.

I thought by discovering exactly what he wanted me to do, I could save our wavering marriage. After years of trying to please someone whose whims changed daily, I realized I'd taken on an impossible task. The problem wasn't my activities, but rather an unhappiness that had sprouted within him. No matter what I did, this unhappy man was not satisfied.

Looking back on that situation, I realize my sense of power was not coming from the right source. I was trying to tune into my husband rather than seeking direction from the Lord.

After hearing Wightman's analogy, I vowed to be more like the arrow in the crossbow, attuned to the real Source of power. Then I would have the strength to do what God called me to do. If I am content to go where God's skillful eye directs me, then I will stay on course.

No one praises the arrow that fells the deer; it is the archer who receives the glory. So should it be with us. When God works through us to accomplish His deeds, we should give the glory to Him as the source of our power. He determines our effectiveness.

How do we allow God to pull the bow string? By studying His Word and turning to Him in prayer, we can seek His guidance for our everyday activities.

God created us to be His messengers, not to be blown by the wind. His divine power has given us all the tools we need to live. — S.T.O.

"I will instruct you and teach you in the way you should go; I will counsel you and watch over you."
PSALM 32:8

Lord,
help us to learn how to be tuned into You so that You may be
our Source of power. Teach us to be content to go where Your
skillful eye guides us. In Jesus' name, Amen.

*

Broken Communication

I do not like crises, but I do like the opportunities they supply.
WILLIAM BARCLAY

Have you ever failed one of your children at a time when he or she desperately needed you? That is what I did—I totally failed my daughter, the person I love most in all the world. Even worse, I was completely unaware of what I had done.

My daughter had a major operation and needed someone to be with her and help her physically and emotionally. My offers to help were met with, "No, I'm OK. I don't need you!"

She asked one of her cousins to come and help her. Thinking that was what she wanted, I left her alone. She became angry and resentful that I wasn't conscious of her outer and inner pain.

Now I realize I should have gone regardless of what she said. The pressure and stress of my own job blinded my eyes. I was shocked when I finally saw the hurt reflected on her face because I had not been there for her. I felt helpless, knowing I was powerless to reverse the situation or correct my failure.

As I witnessed her agony, I blinked hard to keep back my tears. How could I have been so insensitive and uncaring? Could I ever find a way to make things right again?

The morning after I realized the situation, feeling devastated, I opened my Bible and randomly searched through the Psalms for comfort. David's cry for help in Psalm 51 caught my attention. The horror of David's wrongdoing blocked out everything else. All he could think of was his sin. I readily identified with him.

Knowing God was loving and compassionate, David cried out for relief from his guilt and his heavy heart. He knew he could do nothing to alter the circumstances. Any change had to come from within himself.

David came to God, broken and humble. He begged God to forgive him and to cleanse him. Then he asked God to bring back his joy. At last David sensed freedom from his failure. Peace again filled his heart.

David relied on God's faithfulness. I had to do the same. Confessing my sin, I cried out to God, asking for His forgiveness. In His faithfulness, God forgave me, renewed me, and eased my hurting heart. Hope and joy welled up inside me again.

Have you failed one of your children? Read Psalm 51 thoughtfully. Share David's feelings, and pray, seeking forgiveness and restoration. Then go to your child and ask for forgiveness. Don't wait to renew the love between you.

In the future, if your children need help, don't wait to be asked. Let them know you are there for them and that they can depend on you.

God can turn circumstances around to benefit you both. He can bring you out of failure into His peace and joy. He did exactly that for me! The next time my daughter was ill, I took time to care for her. God restored our communication. — L.M.

"Create in me a pure heart, O God, and renew a steadfast spirit within me. Restore to me the joy of your salvation and grant me a willing spirit, to sustain me."

PSALM 51:10, 12

Father,
please help me to be open and responsive when my child is
hurting. Teach me to be sensitive to her present needs, so I
can respond with understanding and love. Amen.

✳

Just Out of Reach

It is never too early to begin blessing someone—even a
difficult person—but we never know when it is too late.
JOHN TRENT

During a seminar, John Trent discussed the Old Testament blessing and how many people today miss out on receiving their parents' blessings. Even if we've moved thousands of miles away or haven't lived at home in many years, we may still feel chained to our past. Missing out on that blessing can affect our entire lives.

He told us his daughter, Carrie, loved to go to the mall with him when she was three. One of her favorite things to do was to place a nickel in the gum ball machine, flip the handle, and grab a candy treat.

John said, "One day, she put a nickel in a gum ball machine and pulled the handle, but nothing happened. I gave her another nickel, and she tried again, but the machine was broken. How do you explain to a three-year-old who has received candy from this gum ball machine time after time, that she cannot have any more candy? She was so close, but she could not receive the gum ball."

I thought of a parallel in my own life. I spent a fortune emotionally putting nickels in a gum ball machine but never getting anything out of it. I felt so close to receiving my mother's blessing, but I never obtained it.

No matter what I did when I was growing up, she wanted more or something different. I was an honor roll student, but she said, "Why can't you get all A's like your friend, Chris." When I was chosen for National Honor Society, I thought, *Now, she will be pleased.* She wasn't. Instead, she said, "Why don't you go out more often? Won't anybody ask you for a date?" That summer, I dated thirty-two guys. Looking back, I see how much time and energy I wasted, trying to please my mother.

As an adult, I always told my mother when I received an award or succeeded in accomplishing something. She seemed disinterested. When my first book was published, I gave her one of the first autographed copies. She never read it. She has never read anything I have written.

It wasn't until I went through my divorce that I began to understand Mother. I realized she was not able to give me a blessing, because she didn't know how to receive one. Although she was attractive and bright, she had suffered a lifetime of low self-esteem. She sought her identity in material possessions, in wealth, in position. Since she was not happy with herself, she could not be pleased with an outgoing daughter who always tried to be a super-achiever.

A year ago, Mother suffered a massive stroke. She cannot walk; she cannot talk—nor will she ever be able to. She will never be able to give me the blessing I have sought. However, I am the one who has changed. I no longer seek her blessing. Instead, I offer mine. It took a long time to apply to my mother what John taught me about "the blessing." Today, I visit and take her special treats. I sit and hold her hand and tell her that I love her. Sometimes, I take her for a surprise outing.

I don't try to impress her with my latest accomplishments. Instead, I just try to be there for her, blessing her, expecting nothing in return—and that's enough. — S.T.O.

> "Esau said to his father, 'Do you have only one
> blessing, my father? Bless me too, my father!'
> Then Esau wept aloud."
> GENESIS 27:38

Lord,
you are my fullness of life. You bless me and fill my cup to
overflowing. In return, I am able to bless others—even those
who are difficult to bless. Amen.

✳

Silence the Loneliness

This soul hath been alone on a wide wide sea:
So lonely 'twas that God Himself
Scarce seemed there to be.
SAMUEL TAYLOR COLERIDGE

Shirley and her husband had separated. After many lonely days and nights, Shirley looked for companionship with people in her same situation. This brought her to our church's Single Parent Fellowship.

One evening she said to me, "I ache inside for someone to understand, someone who will reach out to me. My children are adults with busy careers of their own. They have little time either to listen or to help me cope with my empty life. I feel so lonely."

Loneliness is one of the hardest obstacles we have to conquer in our singleness. We may sit in a crowd, with people on every side, and yet feel lonely. When that special person in our lives is gone, it is difficult to cope with empty feelings that overwhelm us.

Perhaps you have driven down the street with the radio set on your favorite station. When you hear a song from your past, tears stream down your cheeks. Going to a former favorite restaurant brings back a flood of memories. Does seeing old friends, who recall good times from the past, become painful? Do you fight to control your emotions? Many things trigger our minds and bring back experiences we do not want to face because they cause pain and sorrow.

What do you do? How do you accept the fact that you are now single and must make a "go" of your life alone? How can you cope when the need to be with someone overwhelms you? How do you pick up the pieces of your shattered life and rebuild something stable?

Our single parent group provided classes to help Shirley look realistically at her situation so she could begin her healing process. She became involved in various social and church-related activities and found enjoyment in new friends with similar interests.

Through the help and prayers of others, Shirley began to seek the Lord's presence in her life. She became aware that Jesus understood her loneliness. He brought her relief and comfort. Today she is a changed person.

Have you allowed yourself to be caught in the net of loneliness, thinking there is no way out? One way to escape is to contact churches near you to locate a single parent group. Find out if they offer classes that can help meet your needs. Begin attending—become involved. Soon you will find your life turning around as Shirley did.

Remember that our Lord also went through times when He felt forsaken. He empathizes, He cares and understands, and He is *always* with you. — L.M.

> "Surely I will be with you always,
> to the very end of the age."
> MATTHEW 28:20

Father God,
help me to remember that I never walk alone. You have
provided the most wonderful Companion in the world to
walk beside me. Thank you. Amen.

✳

The Step Between

Faith is the step between promise and assurance.
LIFE APPLICATION BIBLE

One of my favorite single moms in the Bible is the widow of Zarephath in chapter 17 of 1 Kings. The only food the widow possessed was a handful of flour in a jar and a little oil. There was a drought in the land, and she honestly believed that she and her son were going to die of starvation. She didn't know where to find their next meal.

It can be hard for single moms to try to envision where the money will come from to sustain them and their children. Their incomes are often drastically reduced by the death of a spouse or the death of a marriage.

Once I saw a cartoon that showed a person anxiously awaiting the reply of a loan officer as he reviewed a request for a home loan. The loan officer asked, "Do you have any collateral except the book inside of you?"

After my divorce, a similar experience caused me to identify with that cartoon. I needed to refinance my house in order to purchase my ex-husband's share. The loan officer said, "You seem to have enough income, but you need to substantiate last year's earnings so we can estimate your future income."

Since my divorce eight years ago, I've owned my own editorial and writing business. In addition, I teach one day a week at a local Christian college, and I'm editor of a monthly magazine. Anyone who looks at my crazy work schedule and erratic 1099's would wonder how I survive—but I do. When I look too far down the road, I question my own logic.

God doesn't show us how our lives will unfold in the future. However, He assures us of His continuous presence. Whenever I ask the Lord if my vocation is in His will, I feel confident that it is.

Elijah instructed the widow to share her bread with him even though there was barely enough for her and her son. When Elijah told her his instructions came from the Lord, she obeyed, and her flour and oil were supplied throughout the drought. She stepped out in faith, confident that God would provide for her even though she didn't know how.

Estimating my income has always been difficult. I often find myself wondering where my next house payment will come from, but somehow the money has always been there. — S.T.O.

For the jar of flour was not used up and the jug of oil
did not run dry, in keeping with the word of the Lord
spoken by Elijah.
1 KINGS 17:16

Dear Lord,
thank You for providing when we see no possible way.
Strengthen our faith that we may obey with the assurance
that You will always supply our needs. Amen.

✳

A Cry for Acceptance

There is no surprise more wonderful than the surprise of
being loved; it is God's finger on man's shoulder.
CHARLES MORGAN

How could I possibly be acceptable to God? No one else
has ever accepted me—why should He?" The cry came
from Helen, a newly divorced woman with deep emotional hurts. "My parents always rejected me. After I was
married, I never felt loved. My husband put me down at
every opportunity. As my boys grew older, they treated
me the same way. No one cared, so how could I ever think
that God loves and accepts me?"

Have you been there? I have. Each of us desires to be
accepted, but often that human need is not satisfied. An
even *deeper* relationship we crave is one with God, our
Heavenly Father. Something inborn within us cries out
for His acceptance—to *know* He loves and cares for us,
and that we are special to Him.

If we have been put down again and again, we believe
we are not worthy of anyone's attention, particularly
God's. This false assumption erodes our thoughts and
emotions and draws us into a downward spiral of despair
and defeat.

That is exactly where Helen was. She decided that
God was uncaring and too distant to hear her cries. She

assigned herself to a life without hope and stifled her recovery with this damaging attitude.

In His Word, God tells us how precious we are. He said, "I have engraved you on the palms of my hands" (Isa. 49:16). He tells us not to fear because He is always present. We belong to Him.

Scripture after scripture reveals His offer of personal, never-ending love. Like Helen, we may be afraid to accept His gift, unwrap it, and make it our own.

How can we experience His wonderful gift? Search God's Word for affirmation of His love. Write down appropriate verses and claim them. Read them aloud over and over until they are lodged in our minds and hearts.

Then, set aside quality time to sit quietly and relax in His presence. He said, "Be still, and know that I am God" (Ps. 46:10). Allow His peace and calm to invade your thinking. Listen until you learn to recognize His voice. It may thunder through your mind, or it may whisper softly to you.

We seldom allow ourselves time to be still in the depths of our being and to wait for awareness of God. When we do, we find that He is there, waiting for us!

Hopefully, Helen will be able to work past her feelings of rejection and reach out to God and to others with a new appreciation of herself.

"Helen, dear friend, you *are* a person of worth. Accept that! He loves you with a never-ending love. Remember that always. Your family and friends will sense the change in you as you begin to blossom in God's love." — L.M.

"Do not fear, for I have redeemed you; I have called you by name; you are mine."
ISAIAH 43:1, NASB

Father,
it is hard at times to believe that You accept and care for me.
Let Your personal love toward me teach me that I am
precious in Your sight. Amen.

✳

An Unlikely Candidate

Attempt great things for God—
Expect great things from God.
WILLIAM CAREY

The most unlikely candidate for the office of apostle was the tax collector, Matthew. The Jews' hatred of tax collectors was great and violent, fueled by their religious conviction that God alone, not Augustus Caesar, was King.

When Matthew followed Jesus without hesitation, he paid a unique price. The other disciples were fishermen and could return to their nets, but when Matthew left his tax office, he could never go back. Matthew took only one thing—his pen, or more precisely, his skill at writing and keeping records. Ultimately, he used that talent to compose the most quoted Gospel in Christian literature.

You, too, may feel like an unlikely candidate to serve God. If your world has been torn apart by death or divorce, you cannot return to life as it was. Like Matthew, you may have reached a point of no return. Plus, your financial situation may have taken a turn for the worse.

You can learn a valuable lesson from Matthew. You may find yourself in a situation where your values are in danger of being compromised by your association with someone. Should you stay? If you remain, you might show acceptance of behavior that goes against your values.

If you find yourself in an uncomfortable situation, walk away. Rely on the strength of Jesus, not your own.

Perhaps Matthew had met Jesus before. Maybe he was thinking about his unethical work and unfulfilled life. Whatever his thoughts, Matthew did not hesitate when Jesus called. He stood up and followed, leaving his past life behind.

Mark and Luke referred to Matthew as Levi, but he called himself Matthew, which means "Gift of Yahweh." Yahweh is the Hebrew name for God.

God has a plan for each of our lives. The only way He can use us to the fullest extent is when we are willing to sacrifice everything and follow Him. Normally, He doesn't ask us to give up material possessions but rather the importance we have placed on them. If we place Him first in our lives, then we, too, can become a "Gift of God."

From his Gospel, we can tell that Matthew found fulfillment and contentment as a disciple of Jesus. If you are willing to follow Jesus, then you'll find a peace and joy in life that you never knew before. — S.T.O.

"As Jesus went on from there, he saw a man named
Matthew sitting at the tax collector's booth.
'Follow me,' he told him,
and Matthew got up and followed him."
MATTHEW 9:9

Dear Lord,
although we might not consider ourselves likely candidates to
be chosen by You, You have chosen each of us to serve You.
Help us to determine our skills that we may use them to
glorify Your name. Amen.

✳

Coping with Windy Days

CHAPTER THREE

We need to "batten down the hatches" when cold and windy days prevail. Sailing through the storms helps us to cope with problems and devastating events. We can find joy in the midst of our circumstances if we surrender our problems to the Lord. Rejection can be overcome, survival resources can be found, and enabling strength is ours in the midst of the turbulence. During these difficult times, God often brings friends into our lives to help share our burdens. Although He allows us to fall into deep valleys, He will lift us to the mountain top where we can learn to trust in His love.

*

The Incapacitating Stroke

You can never do a kindness too soon because you never know
how soon it will be too late.
AUTHOR UNKNOWN

Mother has suffered a stroke. She can't speak, and she is paralyzed on her right side. The doctors don't know if she will survive or not." My sister's words rang in my head as I played them again hoping somehow I had misunderstood the message on my answering machine.

As our parents age, these are words we all fear hearing. Yet, many of us must cope with the health problems of our parents as well as our own concerns and those of our children. When a crisis strikes, it seems doubly difficult if we must carry the burden alone as single parents.

When my mother awoke that fateful Saturday morning, she felt fine. She never dreamed that at 11:15 A.M. she would suffer a massive brain hemorrhage that would change her life of luncheons, bridge foursomes, painting lessons, and beauty salon appointments—forever.

God never promised that we would always enjoy perfect health. He only promised that He would never leave us—that no matter what happened, He would stand by our side ready to uphold and comfort us.

After hearing of Mother's stroke, I anxiously flew to Arizona. It was painful to see her lying in that hospital bed, being fed intravenously—unable to focus her eyes, unable to sit up.

I prayed that she would live and that God would give me the wisdom to know how to pray. For years, she had experienced many ghosts in the closets of her mind. I could find no way to help her set them free. I prayed that

God would heal her troubled heart, that He would grant her the peace for which she had been searching.

I thought of that prayer almost a year later when I returned from a more pleasant visit with my mother. She still could not walk, nor carry on a conversation. However, she was eating well, and she could maneuver her electric wheelchair around with her left hand. The nurses laughingly claimed she was a road hazard in the halls of her nursing home, and sometimes they had to turn the motor of the wheelchair off.

Today, she paints with her left hand, and her therapist framed one of her creations. Every time she says a new word, she is praised. Again she has hope. The ghosts in the closets of her mind no longer haunt her.

When I visit her, I usually take a gift. Once I asked if she wanted some flowers. She shook her head no. She hadn't eaten the last box of chocolates I took.

I asked her, "What can I bring you?"

She smiled and pointed to me. The gift she wanted was my companionship. As single parents, our schedules become incredibly busy, and the greatest gift we can offer a loved one is ourselves—our time. — S.T.O.

"The Lord Himself goes before you and will be with you; He will never leave you nor forsake you. Do not be afraid; do not be discouraged."
DEUTERONOMY 31:8

Lord,
you never promised us perfect health. Help us to comfort our
loved ones when they are ill. No matter what happens, You
stand by our side ready to uphold and comfort us. Amen.

✳

Surviving the Gales

True faith does not look at the obstacles, but rather at God.
DONALD GREY BARNHOUSE

I had no intention of moving after thirty-two years in the same house, but God had other plans. A beautiful mobile home was for sale at an unbelievable price. When I walked into it, I thought, *It's home!*

When I moved in, there was a mouse in the kitchen, the wooden cabinets in back had termites, and I was invaded by ants. I caught the mouse; exterminators came for the termites; I sprayed the ants.

When the final moving day came, my daughter, her boyfriend, and several others came to help. It was the hottest weekend we'd had all summer. A service man came to turn on the air conditioning.

Twenty minutes later, the main sewer line of the park backed up into the bedrooms, bathrooms, utility room, and hallway. Everything had to be moved out of the master bedroom into other rooms. Fortunately, I hadn't unpacked much. Boxes were stacked everywhere! In climbing over rugs and blowers, I hit my foot on the wall and broke my little toe.

After the plumber cleaned out the sewer line, I turned on the air conditioning again. Another flood and another plumber. While the second plumber was there, I asked him to check the toilet in the master bathroom because it was wobbly. He found that it was sinking into the floor because of a longtime leak! This meant a new floor, plus a new toilet. "Please also check the hot water heater," I requested. It, too, was sinking from leakage. More new flooring and a new water heater.

When I did a load of wash, hot, soapy water backed up into the showers and bathtub. The park manager had another plumber come. The third plumber discovered that a stake had been pounded into the ground which had pierced the main sewer line.

Several days later, everything had to be moved outside for the new carpet to be installed.

There were other minor things: the dishwasher quit, a new answering machine didn't work, a full china cabinet shelf came loose, a newly installed faucet had a small drip.

However, from the first happening, I knew God had allowed all of this. He was in control. There was stress, naturally, but I knew He was there. What a blessing my new home was when everything was in its place, and I began to enjoy God's love gift to me. That is what I feel my mobile home is.

Even in the midst of the "gales" that hit my house, the foundation of my faith remained steady and solid, because I know my Father loves me and allowed everything to happen for my ultimate good. — L.M.

"Dear friends, do not be surprised at the painful trial you are suffering, as though something strange were happening to you. But rejoice that you participate in the sufferings of Christ, so that you may be overjoyed when His glory is revealed."

1 PETER 4:12–13

Father,
as the gales subside, I realize Your hand is guiding through
each wave. Thank You for Your care and protection. I love
You. Amen.

∗

Lean into the Wind

Only when we move from the safe harbor of theory to the world of reality, do we actually make a difference.
AUTHOR UNKNOWN

As I scanned the horizon, my eyes focused on a sailboat gliding out of the bay. The boat cruised smoothly for a while, but then, the wind changed direction. The mainsail flapped uselessly in the breeze, and the boat slowed to a near halt. The boat's pilot turned the rudder and guided his craft back into the wind. The sails caught the breeze and filled, and soon the vessel glided swiftly out of the harbor.

While I watched the sailor fight the wind, I thought of a parallel in my own life. I had been working through a situation that caused inner turmoil and suffering. I felt like that mainsail, flapping in the wind with no sense of direction. When my husband of twenty-two years was suddenly no longer a part of my life, feelings of inadequacy and dozens of unanswerable questions filled my mind.

Then there was the adjustment of trying to balance a career, make ends meet, and still find the time to be a good mother to my two sons. It made for long work days that left me tired and resentful. I longed for those happier, calmer days when I wasn't fighting the wind or battling my inner pain. Why had my world suddenly changed? Anger sapped my strength. In frustration, I lashed out at God, "Lord, take this hurt away. Why have these things happened to me?"

Nevertheless, the situation remained unchanged, my questions went unanswered. God seemed silent and unreachable. I kept racing around, fragmented and torn, never pausing to listen to the still, small voice of God within me.

However, after a period of time, a remarkable thing happened. Instead of mentally avoiding the problems in my life and blaming God, I decided to take a different approach. Perhaps what I had assumed to be God's lack of concern was actually my lack of ability to listen to God. I learned to lean into the pain instead of avoiding or fighting it.

Like that sailboat slanting back into the wind, I deliberately decided to find joy in the midst of my circumstances. Instead of asking God to remove my problems, I prayed that He would stand by me throughout the ordeal. Then I took the time to listen for His reply. I found time to spend in His Word each day in spite of my busy schedule.

Although I was still a single parent, juggling finances, career, and teenagers, I no longer felt overwhelmed. Depending on His strength to guide me brought the peace that I'd been seeking. — S.T.O.

"Consider it pure joy, my brothers, whenever you face trials of many kinds, because you know that the testing of your faith develops perseverance."
JAMES 1:2–3

Dear God,
please guide me during the difficult circumstances of my life.
Help me to lean into Your strength where I may find peace
and joy. Amen.
∗

Let Go of Her!

Prayer is the frame of the bridge from weeping to doing,
built across the canyon of despair.
JAMES GILLIOM

I slumped against the hospital wall outside my four-year-old daughter's room. Nurses had snatched her away and thrust her limp body into an oxygen tent.

Earlier, when I arrived at the preschool to pick her up after work, I was told she didn't feel well. I wasn't prepared for the sight of Thelma's chalk-white face with dark circles under her eyes. Her labored breathing evidenced an asthma attack.

The staff had strict instructions to call immediately if this ever happened. But Thelma had lain there several hours, and no one phoned.

Quickly, I gathered my drooping daughter in my arms and raced to the doctor's office. Her breathing difficulty increased. Taking one look at Thelma, the doctor ordered an injection. Her face turned black, her body convulsed, and she vomited.

The nurse phoned the hospital immediately and ordered a room with oxygen. Unable to wait for an ambulance, I drove her myself.

Moments later, standing in Thelma's room, I felt completely helpless. "Mommy, Mommy, don't leave me!" Her white lips formed the words through the haze of the oxygen tent. Her glazed eyes begged for reassurance. She tried to raise her arms.

The nurse signaled that I could sit beside her. One soft, white hand slipped into mine for a few moments before the nurse tucked it back under the tent.

As the nurses worked with her, her breathing gradually became easier. Her small body began to relax. At last the head nurse said, "Ms. Moses, there's nothing you can do. It's better if you don't stay—for her and you. We won't know anything until the crisis passes. Try not to worry. She's in good hands."

I stumbled out to my car, knowing my daughter was "deathly ill." I poured out my heart to God. "Please, Father, don't take her. She's all I have. I love her so much."

"Give her to Me," a quiet voice spoke in my heart.

"No!" I cried. "I can't! She's mine. Don't ask that."

"Let go of her," came the calm, steady voice. "I love her, too. Surrender her to Me."

In desperation, I sobbed, "All right. She's Yours, but please don't take her. Make her well." My reply was not what God wanted. Finally, broken and defeated, I said, "She's in Your hands. Do whatever You will, but if You take her, please help me to bear it!" My head dropped to my chest. My arms fell lifeless in my lap.

I sat quietly, completely drained. Then, suddenly, mysteriously, a deep, penetrating calm washed over my entire being. Worry and panic were replaced by a sense of God's presence and love. I slept peacefully in total faith and trust.

The next day I found a completely different little girl sitting under the oxygen tent. The arms stretched out to me were not limp. Her eyes danced in a face now flushed with color. Her voice was strong with joy and delight at my presence.

What if I had not surrendered her to God? The head nurse had not known how true her words were, "She's in good hands." She's been there ever since. — L.M.

"The Lord was my stay.
He brought me forth also into a broad place;
He rescued me, because He delighted in me."

PSALM 18:18–19, NASB

Father,
when I resist letting go of what I hold as precious, teach me
how to release it into Your hands. Amen.

✳

Don't Give Up

Do what you can with what you have where you are.
TEDDY ROOSEVELT

Thump! The packet the postman pushed through the mail drop landed on the floor. I looked at it and instinctively knew what that brown envelope meant. As a freelance writer, I was accustomed to receiving such packets. Slim envelopes elated me because they carried checks. The thick ones broke my heart. This was a thick one."

The above paragraph was written by Biju Cherian, a student in my writing seminar at the India Communications Institute in Bombay. Although he lives halfway around the world, his message is universal.

Receiving rejection slips is common to my profession of freelance writing, but they are heartbreaking. Authors joke about wallpapering their offices with them or re-using the backs for new ideas.

I have also experienced the sting of rejection since becoming a single parent. How about you, have you felt it? Has your spouse walked out on you? Does your child blame you for the changes that have taken place in your family? Do you feel deserted by family members or former friends? The "thump" of rejection, in any form, can be devastating.

What rejection does to our emotions is not as important as what we do about our situation.

Biju also wrote, "Through the years in my walk with Jesus Christ, I have learned the valuable lesson that the greatest crime is not in making mistakes but in giving up trying."

It takes more courage to press on and to face a challenge with action than it does to sit still and make no mistakes. Before I send out a manuscript, I make a list of all the places it could be sold. Then if it lands in my mail drop, I try to determine why it was rejected and then send it to the next editor on my list.

When I feel rejected by a family member, I try to determine why. If it is a situation that I can remedy, I listen and try to work things out. If rejection comes from someone who is unwilling to deal with the situation, I've learned to leave it in God's hands and pray for that person. Then I get on with my life. It does no good to dwell on past mistakes or on what might have been. The important thing is to press on. — S.T.O.

> "I press on to take hold of that for which Christ Jesus took hold of me."
> PHILIPPIANS 3:12

Dear Lord,
teach me to learn from rejection, rather than to retreat from it. Help me press on and face the challenges which I meet in life, looking to you for my strength. Amen.

✳

Abiding Amidst Rebellion

Great emergencies and crises show us how much greater our
vital resources are then we had supposed.
WILLIAM JAMES

Ron, my son, was only sixteen when his father passed away. Being a teenager, Ron depended on his dad, and he became angry when he died. He felt his father had failed him by leaving him." Ruth sat across the table from me and poured out her story.

"Ron became resistant to everything. He wouldn't talk to me or anyone else; he totally rebelled. He bailed out of high school and failed every class. I forced him to go to church with me, but he closed his ears and wouldn't listen. Instead, he became sullen and withdrawn."

"How did you handle that?" I asked.

"The only thing that kept me going was the absolute conviction that God loved me more than anyone else in the world loved me. Because I was convinced of that, I believed God would not allow anything to happen to me that was out of His control."

"I agree with you, Ruth," I said. "Everything that happens in our lives, good or bad, is under God's control. He can use it to His own purpose and glory."

"Yes," Ruth agreed. "I have a motto on my wall that states, 'God's will, nothing more, nothing less, and nothing else.' That plaque has really helped me.

"It hurts to see my son so rebellious, but I trust God. I put Ron in His hands, knowing that in His time and in His way, God will reach my son. Through the years I tried to remain patient and loving with him, but he still remained closed up inside."

"Has he changed today?" I questioned.

"It took at least seven years before Ron could cope with his father's death," Ruth continued. "He still is not following the Lord, but at least most of the anger is gone. He is finally getting on with his life. There will always be an empty place in his heart which no other man can fill—only his Heavenly Father."

I listened to Ruth with admiration and then remarked, "You seem to have an inner joy in spite of the sorrow you must have felt through the years."

Her face glowed and she smiled at me. "I do," she stated simply. "My joy comes from holding onto the Lord. He said that He is the Vine and I am a branch. I feel as though He has allowed me to wrap myself around Him, and He has held me steady through every storm, protecting me from the winds and rain. I also believe He uses hard things to bring out my inner resources and to make me stronger."

Ruth paused and then added, "I look forward to the day Ron will find that same joy and steadiness."

"I'm certain that day will come," I said as I reached over to hug my friend. — L.M.

"I am the vine, you are the branches; he who abides in Me, and I in him, he bears much fruit; for apart from Me you can do nothing."
JOHN 15:5, NASB

Father,
entwine Your arms tenderly around me. Encourage me to be
strong and hold tightly to You in all the storms of life. Amen.

✳

On the Mat

A Christian is one who makes it easier
for others to believe in God.
AUTHOR UNKNOWN

In Luke 5, the story is told of a paralytic who was healed by Jesus after being lowered through the roof of a house. We don't know much about the man—if he could talk, if he even wanted to be healed. All we know is that Jesus healed him because of the faith of his friends.

Do you identify with the man on the mat? Maybe you have recently gone through a divorce, and your spirits are low. You may feel like all the props have been knocked out from under you, and you are on the mat.

Women react to such circumstances in various ways. Some place a veneer around themselves and pretend nothing is wrong. Others build a thick, impenetrable wall shutting out even their friends and family members because of the hurt. Pain can incapacitate a single mother, causing her to become paralyzed like the man on the mat. During those times, it becomes difficult to see Jesus.

Just before making the divorce decision, I was at a low point in my life. My mind was fragmented and clouded by stress and indecision. Sometimes I couldn't even pray.

Today, people ask me, "How did you cope during that time? How did you survive your darkest moment?"

I reply, "People. God brought unexpected angels into my life who could see through the smile pasted on my face. They realized when I said, 'I'm fine,' that I was actually hurting."

Several of my friends understood what was happening in my life even before I did. One couple invited me to dinner, to the theater, and to church functions on a regular basis. Actually, they dragged me. This occurred even before I had made the divorce decision. I was often home alone and lonely on weekends while my husband traveled.

Another friend was there to listen, and anything I said would be kept in strictest confidence. Up to that point, I was hesitant to share my problems with anyone. I was still hoping for a reconciliation with my husband, who was a very private person. He would have been crushed if I had told others and then we had worked things out.

At that time in my life, I was so stressed I could not even read the Bible. When I tried, my vision blurred. My mind was such a jumble that the thoughts behind the words made no sense. Nevertheless, I forced myself to read it, even when I was not able to gain any encouragement or insight from God's Word.

Pain and uncertainty paralyzed me. I knew God would heal me, like He did the paralytic, if I could only reach Him. However, I wasn't sure how to get to that point.

Like the man on the mat, my friends made it possible for me to see Jesus. I saw Him through the concern in the eyes of Christians who helped me cope with my difficult circumstances. — S.T.O.

> "When Jesus saw their faith, he said,
> 'Friend, your sins are forgiven.'"
> LUKE 5:20

Dear Lord,
we thank You for friends and for their faith. Because of these
friends, we have a window to You, even in our most difficult
circumstances. Amen.

✳

Wings to Soar

I've topped the wind swept heights with easy grace where
never lark nor eagle ever flew.
JOHN GILLESPIE MAGEE, JR.

Pandemonium broke out in the nest! The day arrived when the mother eagle decided her eaglets were ready to try their wings. Her babies were *not* in agreement.

She had built her nest high in the mountains among the rocks. Instinctively, she knew the danger. If one of her young fell from the nest before learning to fly, it could drop thousands of feet and be crushed.

The young eaglets, encased in warmth and security, did not want to be disturbed in their daily routine; but today everything changed.

Their mother removed the cozy cushioning and forced them out of their nest. One after another, she pushed them over the side. Angry squawking and screeching accompanied this action. Finding themselves falling, they frantically flapped their weak, inexperienced wings. Mother eagle swooped grandly below them, spreading out her own strong wings.

As the young birds tired, they dropped safely onto a broad, feathery cushion. Then, upward the mother eagle soared, putting them through the same process again and again. Eventually, their wings developed strength, and they began to fly on their own. What fun they had—gliding through the air, over the mountains, into the valleys, catching the air currents. The mother felt satisfaction as she watched each eaglet gain strength and confidence.

Many centuries ago, Moses compared a mother eagle's love for her young to God's love for His people. The comparison from this beautiful example still holds true today.

Sometimes God allows pandemonium in our homes, and we fail to remember His great love for us. He prods us out of our security so we can try our wings. When we teeter on the edge of the nest, we may become fearful and "screech." We need assurance that our Father's mighty arms are outstretched to catch us when we fall. He will raise us up to fly again and again until we grow strong. Unlike the young eaglets, we will *always* need our Father's presence, no matter what our age or circumstances.

Although God pushes us out of our comfort zone and allows us to fall into the deep valleys, He also lifts us up to dwell on the mountain tops. From there we can catch the air currents of His love and soar in the skies with Him.

What delight He has when we finally increase in strength and grow confident enough to spread our wings and fly. Even then He is there, challenging us to climb higher by trusting His love. — L.M.

"Like an eagle that stirs up its nest, That hovers over its young, He spread His wings and caught them, He carried them on His pinions."
DEUTERONOMY 32:11, NASB

Father,
even though I resist leaving my comfort zone, I know Your mighty wings support me. May I always be encouraged and confident to soar in the heights with You. Amen.

✳

Life After Death

CHAPTER FOUR

We grow through the difficult circumstances in our lives. God teaches
us to move forward only one step at a
time. He helps us to accept being
alone and to find hope in the midst of
our hopelessness. Shock lessens as we
let go of the past and find new dreams
to replace the old. God promises us
restoration and victory. He promises
resurrection. There is life after death.

*

Can I Make It Alone?

Oh, lonesome's a bad place
To get crowded into.

KENNETH PATCHEN

Darrel and I dated throughout college and married a couple of weeks after graduation. It was exciting," Debbie said as she glanced up at me from under her long lashes. A sorrowful look crossed her face. "You see," she continued, "he was going into the ministry, and I was going to be a teacher. It was what we both wanted. We felt confident we were following God's will—for awhile, anyway.

"Darrel became a youth pastor. However, after a year, there was a messy disagreement among the elders about how things should be handled in the church. Darrel became fed up with the bickering, so he resigned and went into the insurance business instead."

"Was that better for him?" I asked.

"No. He began acting obnoxious like some of the guys he worked with. They influenced Darrel. He decided he wasn't happy, so he left me and took on their lifestyle."

"How long had you been married?"

"Only about three and a half years. During the next three years he became involved with several women, but he kept coming back to me off and on. I still loved him and was stupid enough to allow him to come back each time. During that time our first son was born. Then I became pregnant with our second son. Darrel was scared and left for good."

"Did you see him again?" I questioned.

"Two years later, he wanted to come back. Some woman had dumped him. I told him he could come back

61

only if we went to counseling and only if we were back together this time for good. I knew if he didn't go for counseling, it wouldn't last."

"Did he go?"

"No, he wasn't willing to. Shortly after that he found someone else and left again. After nine years, we finally divorced. I couldn't believe it was happening to me.

"I felt so alone and forsaken when I knew it was final. I feared I would never make it by myself. Even though Darrel had been gone off and on, it was different now, knowing he would never be back. The full responsibility of the boys was mine. We were better off without him, but I felt lonely. I wondered if anyone cared whether I made it or not."

"How did you manage?"

"It wasn't easy. I felt deserted. Gradually, the boys and I began attending church regularly. Because of my hurt, I didn't get close to people at first. I didn't want to open my heart again and allow myself to be rejected. It was easier for the boys. Finally, though, we began cultivating some good friendships."

She smiled. "After awhile, I realized that Jesus had times of great loneliness, too. So now, when I begin having difficult times coping, I sit down with my Bible and open my heart to Him.

"I know He understands. He brings me companionship and comfort. I know now that I am never completely alone. He is always with me." — L.M.

"I will make rivers flow on barren heights, and springs within the valleys. I will turn the desert into pools of water, and the parched ground into springs."
ISAIAH 41:18

Lord,
when I am lonely remind me to turn to You for comfort and
companionship. You fill the thirsty places in my soul with
Your life-giving water. Thank You. Amen.

*

Climbing Out of the Pit

There is no pit so deep that He is not deeper still.
CORRIE TEN BOOM

One morning my husband, looking tired and tense, walked into the kitchen. Deep circles had formed under his eyes. He sat down at the breakfast table and said, "I care about you, but I don't love you enough to live with you anymore."

After twenty-two years of marriage, my world crumbled. I had felt that things weren't quite right between us, but didn't dream that he wanted out of our marriage. We had been going to a Christian counselor for six months, but the marriage was dead. Part of me died with it since so much of my life revolved around my husband.

Emotionally, I fell into a deep pit. I reached a point where I was too stressed to pray and too fragmented to read the Bible. It was impossible for me to reach out and call on God during this period when I needed Him most. God seemed distant and silent.

I wanted my situation changed and my problems solved, although I was unwilling or unable to do anything to alter my circumstances. My poor mental attitude was having a negative effect on my children. They, too, suffered from the pending divorce. Yet, I didn't have the reserves to comfort them or quell their doubts and fears.

There were times when I didn't want to face the future—the next day, the next week, the next year. Even when I didn't have the strength to turn to God, He always helped me through the next five minutes, the next hour, and then the next. During that time, God taught me valuable lessons, but His timing was not my timing. I didn't like the position I was in, but I began to realize that God had placed me there for a reason. In time, I was able to pray again and to listen for His answer.

One step at a time, I began to climb out of the pit. It was not easy. Many times, I lost my footing and slipped backwards. My forward motion often seemed one inch at a time. Eventually I realized that God *had* been there all along, waiting for me to reach out and take His hand. Although He didn't lift me out of the pit, I could sense His presence as I slowly climbed out. Looking back, I now see that God had allowed devastating circumstances to enter my life. Yet, He used each painful situation to strengthen my faith and to help me grow, once I learned to depend on His strength. During this catastrophic experience, I found God's presence and peace in a way I had never known before. — S.T.O.

"He lifted me out of the slimy pit, out of the mud and mire; he set my feet on a rock
and gave me a firm place to stand."
Psalm 40:2

Dear God,
please help me to seek Your presence during the difficult times
when I find it hard to reach out to You. Use each incident in
my life to strengthen my faith. Amen.

✳

Is There Hope Left?

Hope is one of the principal springs that keeps mankind in motion.

ANDREW FULLER

Nora hummed to herself as she planned her upcoming wedding. Even though Joe wasn't all she desired in a husband, she expected to be happy. Suddenly, it seemed as though God spoke in her mind. "What are you doing?"

"Why are You asking me that, God? You know I'm getting remarried. I love Joe. I didn't have any hope until I met him. I can't let him go. He may be my last chance."

Brave words—but they made Nora stop and think about her past. She came from a single parent home and never felt loved as a child. Her mother was too busy to spend time with her. Her mother turned to alcohol, and in her teens, Nora also took up her mother's drinking habits. In spite of her lifestyle, Nora believed in God, but did not know how to develop an intimate relationship with Him.

She met her first husband, Harry, at a time when they both were looking for an escape. His parents drank heavily and had abused him. Because of their similar backgrounds, they were drawn to each other.

However, fourteen years and three children later, their marriage fell apart. Their drinking had escalated into arguments, abuse, and violence. Life became intolerable. Finally, Nora decided she could no longer live that way.

She knew they both shared in the destruction of their marriage. Nora forgave him for all the violence and drinking, until she discovered he had a girlfriend. This she could not forgive, so she filed for divorce.

Her sons felt abandoned and began looking for love in the wrong places. So did Nora. Then she met Joe.

Even though she planned to marry him, she had a gut-feeling he was not the right choice. Now she sensed that God had confronted her. She had to make a decision.

She telephoned Joe and told him it wouldn't work. Within a few months, he married someone else. His behavior became violent toward his new wife, and Nora realized that Joe would have treated her worse than her former husband had.

Was there any hope left for decency in her life? Nora heard about our Single Parent Fellowship and decided to give it a try. She also began attending support groups at the church for recovery from alcohol abuse to help herself and her boys. It was a gradual, difficult process, but she began to sense healthy changes in their lives.

After several months, she said, "I see what God is doing in the lives of other single parents. Is there any possibility He will do the same for me some day?"

The theme song of our Single Parent Fellowship is, "In His Time." Nora has great hope that with God there *is* hope for a renewed life—in His time. However, her first desire is for an intimate fellowship with God. — L.M.

"But seek first His kingdom, and His righteousness, and all these things shall be added to you as well."
MATTHEW 6:33, NASB

Father God,
when my life seems hopeless, help me to remember that You
are the God of Hope, and with You all things are possible. I
place my trust in You. Amen.

✳

The Fatal Fall

Life is a mixture of sunshine and rain,
teardrops and laughter, pleasure and pain.
HELEN STEINER RICE

The manager at the telephone company, where I worked as a service representative, called me into his office. "I just received a call from White River, Arizona. Your father didn't show up at work today. He is missing, and his car was found parked on a mountain road—it was empty."

I collapsed into a chair. A small voice inside told me my father was dead.

He looked at me compassionately. "Why don't you go home? I'll call you when I get more information."

I numbly drove home where I sat by the telephone all afternoon and evening. Finally, the telephone rang the next morning—December 22nd. My manager said, "A scouting group of Apache Indians found your father at the bottom of a two-hundred-foot cliff. I'm sorry, Susan. Let me know if there's anything I can do. Take as much time off as you need."

Although this incident occurred thirty years ago, I remember the conversation and the pain like it happened only yesterday. Daddy and I were always very close. When I was in the fourth grade, I chose my own church. He faithfully drove me there every Sunday until I was old enough to drive.

My father was one of my best friends. We talked openly and honestly with one another. He listened to me and understood my feelings. Daddy encouraged me in my school work and helped me work out my problems. Plus, he taught me to think for myself. When he and my mother divorced after twenty-two years of marriage, it was my turn to listen.

After his death, I received a letter he had written the night before he died. He wrote:

Dear Susan,

Tomorrow is Saturday. I will pack a picnic lunch and hike up a nearby mountain. I'll take some photographs for you and send them in my next letter . . .

Over the next few days, I was able to piece together the details of the accident. Daddy had been hiking along a trail when a ledge of soft limestone gave way beneath him. His camera, with the promised pictures, was found next to him.

It's hard to have a loved one snatched from this earth with no warning, especially when that person is your closest relative.

The weeks and months that followed are a blur in my mind today, but I do remember I turned to God. This was the first time in my life a situation was so overwhelming that I couldn't handle it by myself. The Lord stood by me and upheld me during that difficult time.

Many years later, I, too, went through a divorce. Once again, my most significant loved one was snatched away. This time it was easy to depend on my heavenly Father for my strength.

Over the years, when I have received an award, earned a degree, or had a new book published, my aunts and cousins always say, "Your father would have been so proud of you today."

I feel his presence, loving and encouraging me to be all that God has chosen for me to be. Because of the love

I shared with my earthly father, I've had no trouble loving my Heavenly Father and accepting His love. "Thank you, Daddy, for teaching me well." — S.T.O.

"And I pray that you, being rooted and established in love, may have power, together with all the saints, to grasp how wide and long and high and deep is the love of Christ."
EPHESIANS 3:17–18

Lord,
thank You for the fond memories of the loving relationship I
had with my father. Thank You, too, for the loving
relationship I have with You. Amen.

✳

He Didn't Come Back

Our joys as winged dreams do fly;
Why then should sorrow last?
Since grief but aggravates thy loss
Grieve not for what is past.
THE FRIARS OF ORDERS GRAY

You leave my husband alone! You're breaking up my family. Tend to your own family and leave mine alone!" Evelyn yelled into the phone.

An insidious laugh burst from the other end. "You've got a lot of nerve calling me," the woman's voice answered. "I've no intention of letting go of your husband. We love each other."

"He loves his family," Evelyn responded. "We have two wonderful children. You have no right to wreck *our* home. Who's taking care of *your* children while you're cavorting with my husband?"

"You tend to *your* own business, nosy! If your husband really loved you, he wouldn't be having an affair with me." With that, the phone slammed down.

Evelyn was furious. "Ohhhhh! That woman! If I could get my hands on her, I would throttle her! What does my husband possibly see in her?"

Evelyn was so distraught she couldn't sit down. She picked up a folded newspaper and stormed around her kitchen, pounding everything in sight—the sink, table, washing machine, dryer. Finally, she calmed down.

The affair continued for several months. Eventually, Evelyn's husband packed his clothes and left. Even though Evelyn was devastated, she still had a dream deep in her heart that he would return. In fact, with this hope in mind, she made an appointment with the pastor of their church. The two sets of husbands and wives met with him.

"We received no help from the pastor whatsoever," Evelyn told me. "All he did was ask my husband to resign from his position at church. His new lifestyle was unacceptable. That didn't help me. I still had a home to run and two children to feed and clothe. My husband resigned and took a secular job to help with support."

Evelyn kept praying for God to restore their family. Despite her anger, she pleaded with her husband to come home. The children needed their father.

A year later, the affair ended. One day her husband called and cried over the phone. "Why are you crying?" she asked him sharply. Without giving him a chance to answer, she said, "Because of us? No! You are crying because of what you did. You know it was wrong."

He hung up the phone without saying another word. He never returned home.

Infidelity is one of the hardest situations for women to cope with. It strikes at the very core of our hopes and dreams for a happy, fulfilling life. It is only by reaching out to God for His grace and strength that Evelyn has been able to lead a productive life and find peace. Our Father waits for us to bring our shattered dreams to Him. Do you need to reach out? — L.M.

"So do not fear, for I am with you; do not be dismayed, for I am your God. I will strengthen you and help you; I will uphold you with my righteous right hand."

ISAIAH 41:10

Father,
we have no stamina within ourselves to face the gaping
wounds caused by an unfaithful spouse. We cannot go on
without Your help and strength. Thank You for healing our
wounds. Amen.

✳

Something More

Tell me not, in mournful numbers,
Life is but an empty dream!
For the soul is dead that slumbers,
And things are not what they seem.
HENRY WADSWORTH LONGFELLOW

I have always identified with Martha in the New Testament. She liked to organize things and people—organize them her way. Martha had a plan for her family and for Jesus, but Jesus had other plans.

I'm an organizer, too. I've organized swim meets, women's clubs, and church committees. Like Martha, I had a plan. I enjoyed being a stay-at-home wife and mother, and I began free-lance writing as a hobby. I never intended to develop a full-time career, but the Lord had other plans.

When Lazarus became ill, it was Martha's plan for Jesus to come and heal her brother. She naturally assumed that He would drop everything and come immediately. However, Jesus was late. He disrupted her plan. Martha knew Jesus could heal Lazarus; she knew Lazarus didn't have to die.

When Jesus did not show up according to Martha's timetable, she had to let go of Lazarus. She also had to let go of her plan. Jesus waited until four days after Lazarus had been placed in the tomb before going to Martha. In her frustration, Martha cried out, "Lord, . . . if you had been here, my brother would not have died" (John 11:21).

When my marriage died, I cried, "Change my husband, Lord. Restore this marriage and bring it back to life." I forgot to ask, "Is this marriage in your will, Lord? Do you have other plans for me?"

Like Martha, I like being in a position of control. I thought I was depending on the Lord, but in retrospect, I was using my own energies to accomplish my goals. As long as I wanted to be in control, Jesus could not be. I needed to let go of my plans.

Jesus asked Martha some pointed questions. He asked her if she believed in Him. Martha answered, "Yes, but . . ." Jesus gave her time to ponder before He raised Lazarus from the dead. Then, He gave back something more to Martha than she had before—an understanding of God and of His glory.

To see God's glory in our own lives, we must let go of what we are holding onto. He doesn't want us to reply,

"Yes, but . . . " Our security cannot come from another individual, from a job, or from our own accomplishments.

During my divorce, there were some who said, "You claim to be a Christian. Let's see if you live that out in your own life now that the going is tough." These people needed to see the risen Lord living in my life. The only way I could do this was to die to my own will, to my original hopes and dreams.

As Christians, we are called to receive something special—something that others miss. I needed to let go of my own plans to experience God's plan. — S.T.O.

"Did I not tell you that if you believed,
you would see the glory of God?"
JOHN 11:40

Dear God,
teach us to be willing to give up our own goals and ambitions
to seek Your will. Only then can we experience "something
more" in our lives. Amen.

✳

Rescued and Restored

We need not fear the perils around us so long as the eye of the
Lord is upon us.
AUTHOR UNKNOWN

Betty and her children, Sammy and Suzy, leaned over the fence of her grandfather's farm, watching the shepherd work with his sheep.

Several of the new lambs were wobbling on unsure legs. "Look, Mom, isn't that little one cute? He is so playful," Suzy said, pointing to a small, frisky lamb. "Can I play with it?"

The shepherd nodded his approval, and they all climbed over the fence. Shortly afterwards, the shepherd suddenly shaded his eyes and looked across the fields.

"What are you searching for?" Betty asked.

"One of my ewes," he answered. "She is always getting into trouble. She lays down in a soft burrow, rolls over to get comfortable, then can't get up. That's probably what happened to her. I have to find her before she panics."

"We'll help you look," Betty offered. "Where would she be?"

"Anywhere. Just look for four legs sticking up and pawing the air," he answered. "Holler for me. Don't try to turn her over. She's too heavy for you."

They each took off in a different direction. Before long, Sammy yelled, "I found her. She's over here!"

As soon as the shepherd reached the ewe, he turned her on her side and gently stood her on her feet, bracing her between his legs. He rubbed each of her legs until she could stand by herself.

"You silly thing," he said lovingly, "you've been rescued once again. Now get back where you belong." He released her, and she ambled off toward the rest of the flock.

"What would have happened if we hadn't found her?" Suzy asked.

"She might have suffocated herself," the shepherd answered. "That is why she has to be restored to her feet as quickly as possible."

"Wow!" Sammy exclaimed. "Are there lots of things you have to do for the sheep?"

"Yes, there are, young man. They have to be constantly watched so they don't eat or drink the wrong things. When it's gnat season, I anoint their heads with oil; otherwise they get irritated and pound their heads on the posts. Sheep are not very smart. They need someone to constantly watch over them and protect them."

Betty was quietly thoughtful for a moment, and then she commented, "You know, kids, Jesus said He is our Good Shepherd. Do you suppose He cares for us like that?"

They both looked up, and after a few moments Suzy said, "When we get into trouble, Jesus does the same things for us."

Betty nodded her head. "When things bother us, like having to do something we don't want to do, or we get angry or hurt, Jesus helps us so we aren't irritable. He always watches over us and protects us."

Sammy chimed in, "He really *is* our Good Shepherd, isn't He?" — L.M.

"The Lord is my shepherd, I shall not want. He makes me lie down in green pastures; He leads me beside quiet waters. He restores my soul."
PSALM 23:1–3, NASB

Lord,
thank You for being my Good Shepherd. You watch over all the areas of my life, especially when I'm in danger. You stand me back on my feet and restore me. Thank You. Amen.

✳

Sonya's Legacy
A bird doesn't sing because he has an answer—he sings because he has a song.
JOAN ANGLUND

One day I was talking to my neighbor, Sonya—nothing profound—just chit-chat. The next day she suffered a brain aneurysm and died.

Of all the people in my neighborhood, Sonya appeared the least likely to die. At fifty-eight, she was in excellent health, exercised regularly, and ate all the right foods. There are no easy answers to the question of why someone so vibrant and energetic, so full of life, should suddenly die. But God never promised us all the answers to those kinds of questions.

At her funeral, I looked around the church. I saw neighbors who, to my knowledge, did not have a personal relationship with Jesus Christ. Yet, here they were, paying their respects to our mutual friend, Sonya. I thought of what a witness her life, made possible through her death, was to them.

Her sons, Jeff and Scott, read letters they had written to "Mom." The letters were sorrowful and questioning, yet joyful and comforting. Although these grown sons felt their own pain and loss, they rejoiced that their mother was in heaven with her Savior, Jesus Christ. Their letters were a testimony of how close their family had been.

Jeff's letter stated, "As Peter was the rock upon which Christ built his Church, you were the cornerstone of our family, Mom."

Scott wrote, "We are truly blessed to have experienced such a loving relationship between you and Dad which you poured onto Jeff and me. In fact, it overflowed onto anyone fortunate enough to come across your path. You willingly became involved in countless lives to dynamically change people who in turn will change others. This legacy, created by you, will affect this world forever."

What a wonderful tribute those letters were—to a woman who had always helped others, particularly young people, to become the best they could be. A friend and counselor, she impacted numerous lives. People cried at Sonya's funeral, saddened by her passing. Others were made acutely aware of their own mortality.

How many tomorrows will we face on this earth? We never know. This stark truth was brought home to me that day as I stared at Sonya's casket. Each one of us needs to reflect for a moment and ask, "If I died tomorrow, what kind of legacy would I leave behind?"

Sonya and her family encouraged me for six years during and after my divorce. Now it was my turn to give back some Christian love and concern. — S.T.O.

"For to me, to live is Christ and to die is gain."
PHILIPPIANS 1:21

Dear Lord,
sometimes we are reminded that our hours on this earth are
numbered. Help us to leave behind a legacy that will witness
to others in Your name. Amen.

❋

Joy Blooming

CHAPTER FIVE

As healing begins to take place, we gain fulfillment. Then we can reach out to help others, who will see Christ through our concern and caring as we comfort them. In the process of becoming whole, we find contentment. As we focus our eyes on the Lord, we become who He wants us to be, and He will use us where we are. Joy blooms as we realize we truly are precious to God.

*

Givers and Takers

If someone listens, or stretches out a hand, or whispers a kind word of encouragement, or attempts to understand a lonely person, extraordinary things begin to happen.

LORETTA GIRZARTIS

Can you make it down the stairs?" asked my great-aunt Velma. I nodded yes, and she bounded spryly down the flight of stairs ahead of me.

I laughed at the absurdity of the question. Here she was thirty-plus years my senior, and she was worried about whether I could keep up with her or not.

I thought back to my telephone call to her several weeks earlier when I discovered I would be within a two-hour drive of her nursing home. I hadn't seen Velma in over twenty years, although we had kept in touch. When I had invited her to lunch, I wondered if she was mobile enough to join me, or if the outing would wear her out because of her age. Now after a whirlwind tour of her enormous nursing facility, I was the one who was left dragging behind.

Velma's husband had died a number of years before. Until she retired, she had worked at the same retirement center in which she now lived.

I commented on how nicely decorated her room was. She said, "Oh, I never spend any time in here. There are so many people in the hospital wing who are lonely and need to be visited. Every chance I get, I stop by as many rooms as I have time for."

"Is that how you keep fit—walking from your wing to the hospital wing?" I asked. This was the largest nursing home facility I had ever seen.

"That helps, but I also deliver a newsletter to all the rooms. I get my exercise, and I visit with everyone in the entire center."

Velma is a delightful, energetic woman. Her smile brings sunshine to the many lives she touches daily. She doesn't have a car, and she rarely leaves her nursing home. Yet, she has a fulfilling ministry right outside her doorway. I will treasure the day we spent together.

In my mind, I contrasted this delightful, eighty-plus-year-old woman with the "takers" I had known. Takers obtain from those people around themselves until they drain them. Then they move on. The more they take, the emptier they become, so it becomes a vicious cycle. Their eyes and hearts are centered on themselves, and they are never satisfied.

Givers, like Velma, gain fulfillment by giving themselves to others. Velma doesn't worry about her age, her health, or her loneliness. Her eyes are focused on her Savior and on others to whom she can minister. When others look at Velma, they see Christ ministering through her. — S.T.O.

"The King will reply, 'I tell you the truth, whatever you did for one of the least of these brothers of mine, you did for me.'"
MATTHEW 25:40

Dear Lord,
teach us to be givers like my dear Aunt Velma. Help others to see You through our actions of giving and caring. In Jesus' name, Amen.

✳

Mending Cracks

Open my ears, Lord,
and I will catch the subtle sounds of silent distress.

ELAINE PORCH

One day I was watching a large egg on a TV advertisement. A crack began when something bad was said to it. Another negative comment caused a second crack, and then another. Can you identify with that egg? I do.

For several months I had a situation in my life that produced stress, hurt, and depression. Sometimes I wondered if my friends could hear the shattering inside of me.

You may feel exactly the same way. Things have broken apart in your life—things that affect yourself and your family. There are many happenings in our lives that can cause cracks: serious medical problems, financial crises, divorce, the loss of a spouse or child by death. Fractures can also occur from misunderstandings between family members or friends. How do we mend the cracks?

Let me share a couple of ideas that may help you.

First, when something devastating happens, go immediately to your Heavenly Father in prayer. Too often He is our last resort instead of our first priority. When you talk to Him about the problem, you will find He is there waiting to comfort you. He knows all about the problem and what the solution should be before you even speak. His "mending glue" is incomparable.

Second, look for someone "with skin on" to confide in. In my case, God brought a trusted friend who listened with patient understanding. Her compassionate heart and gentle words helped comfort me and lift my spirit. The stress and depression I had felt began to subside.

When the cracks in our own lives have mended, or are well on their way, we are able to reach out to other hurting individuals who have breaks appearing in their lives. Our experiences enable us to listen, to understand, and to bring comfort.

All of us have times when we need to be encouraged and to encourage—to be lifted up and to lift up others. We need each other, because each of us desires to become whole.

Listen for the cracking. Can you hear it? When you do, stretch out your heart with compassion and offer the glue to help put someone else back together. — L.M.

"Praise be to the God and Father of our Lord Jesus Christ, the Father of compassion and the God of all comfort, who comforts us in all our troubles, so that we can comfort those in any trouble with the comfort we ourselves have received from God."

2 CORINTHIANS 1:3–4 NIV

Father,
you have mended so many cracks in my life.
Make my ears and heart sensitive to the hurts and needs
of others so I can offer comfort and encouragement to them as
You restore them to wholeness. Amen.

*

A Surprise Encounter

Allow God to provide through unexpected encounters.
AUTHOR UNKNOWN

I gazed into the flickering flames of the campfire and settled back in my sand chair with my feet propped up on the picnic table. Our campsite was located on a bluff about fifty yards from the ocean. The surf was rolling in, and foam-capped waves surged on the rocks below.

My friend Nancy threw our last log on the fire. "This location is so relaxing," she said.

"I wish we had brought more wood," I moaned. "I could sit here all night." Getting away for the weekend was exactly what I needed. The balancing act of being a single parent with two sons in college, working full-time, and attending college myself had left me drained. I had not been taking enough time for myself to replenish my energy level.

Here was a chance to roast marshmallows over a fire pit without moving from my sand chair. Plus, it was fun catching up on the news with my dear friend. Watching the fire helped melt the tension out of my tired muscles. For the first time in months, I relaxed.

Suddenly, a cherry-red four-wheel drive pickup screeched to a halt in the campsite next to ours. Eight teenage boys piled out of the pickup and began unloading an assortment of food bags, coolers, and an endless supply of wood. I noticed there were no sleeping bags among their provisions.

Oh, no! I thought to myself. *I bet they are planning to party all night. We'll never get any sleep!*

"Excuse me, Ma'am." A tall blond teen with a ponytail towered over my sand chair, interrupting my thoughts. "We want to run to the general store. Would you be willing to watch our campsite while we're gone?"

"I'd be happy to," I replied.

Grabbing an armful of logs, he continued, "Here. It looks like you're out of firewood. We brought tons. Help yourself to as much as you need."

He hopped back into the cab of his truck while his friends piled into the back. The boys all waved as they drove away.

Nancy and I looked at each other and laughed. We soon had a blazing fire. I settled back into my sand chair to exchange a few more stories with my friend.

The boys *were* up all night long, but they talked softly. I realized they were still there when I awoke in the middle of the night only because I heard their fire crackling.

The next thing I knew it was after 9:00 A.M. As I stumbled out of the camper, the boys were in the process of throwing their coolers and leftover food into the bed of the pickup. They had carefully put out their campfire and had cleaned up the campsite.

The blond young man smiled at me and said, "We don't want our wood. Go ahead and take the rest."

Before leaving, I filled the camper with the remaining wood. Every time I built a fire for months afterwards, I thought of those teenage boys.

How wrong my first impression had been. I was aware that God planned that therapeutic evening. He knew I would run out of wood, and although I hadn't specifically asked Him for more, He provided anyhow. — S.T.O.

"Delight yourself in the Lord, and He will give you the desires of your heart."
PSALM 37:4

Lord,
help me to grasp the opportunities You present in unexpected ways. Often, You use them to provide the desires of my heart.
Thank You. Amen.

✳

An Unmatched Sock

Sweet are the thoughts that savor of content;
The quiet mind is richer than a crown.
ROBERT GREENE

You should have seen me!" my friend Chrys said, laughing. "It was midnight at the end of a long, busy day. I sat at the kitchen table with a monstrous pile of clean laundry in front of me."

"Oh, I can imagine," I commiserated. "You must have a mound of sorting with two children. I would *never* fold clothes at midnight. That's sleeping time."

"I know," Chrys said, "but it was my only free time, and the boys needed clean clothes for school. We straightened their bedroom and rounded up their dirty clothes."

Grinning, I asked, "Did you find them all?"

"I hope so. After I folded everything else, I had a pile of socks to match up. I figured I'd get rid of all the spare ones in their dresser as well, so I dragged those out, too."

"Sounds like a hassle," I said.

"Yes, it really was, and guess what!"

"What?" I asked.

"When I finished matching all the pairs, I had more stray socks than when I started—at least a couple dozen."

"Oh, my!" I groaned. "What did you do?"

"I kept trying to fit some together, but none of them were close in color or design. It was frustrating. Finally, I picked up one of the socks and stared at it. 'You're just like me,' I told it."

"What did you mean by that?" I asked, chuckling.

"Well, I used to be half of a pair, too. I had a mate and we matched. We went everywhere together. Now, since my husband and I are divorced, I am no longer part of a pair. I feel like I've been put in a pile, or in a drawer, with other singles while we all wait for a new mate, just like the lone socks.

"I still think I have a lot of use and wear left in me, but here I am, waiting. At the same time, though, I have some choices."

"What are those, Chrys?" I asked.

"Well, if I really wanted to, I could probably find someone to share my life with, but he might not be the perfect match that God has in mind for me. Therefore, I need to become content in my singleness, waiting on God. I believe it is extremely important for me to first find contentment within myself. When, and if, God has the perfect match for me, He knows where I am.

"In the meantime, I want God to use me like a spare sock—helping others, brushing away dust from their lives, polishing silver linings, wiping up spilled hurts, or keeping a hand or foot warm. There are many ways my creative God can use me if I allow Him.

"Believe it or not, I *am* contented within myself, and it's a wonderful feeling." From her expressionon, I could tell she was sincere. — L.M.

> "I have learned to be content
> in whatever circumstances I am."
> PHILIPPIANS 4:11, NASB

Father,
help me not to feel like an unmatched sock in a drawer.
Instead, teach me to look for possibilities where You can use
me. Thank You. Amen.

✳

His Magnificent Stained Glass Window

You may break, you may shatter the vase, if you will,
But the scent of the roses will hang round it still.

THOMAS MOORE

The vase slipped from my hands and crashed on the kitchen floor. The cut roses lay neatly on the counter, but the crystal urn I had intended to put them in was shattered. I could never mend it.

The long-stemmed red roses were a birthday gift from my oldest son. He knew they were my favorite. His thoughtfulness was intended to help me get through a very difficult day.

As I stared at the broken pieces of glass scattered all over the kitchen floor, it occurred to me that most of us experience times when our lives are splintered like that vase. Some of us lose a family member. Others suffer from illness or severe personal problems.

How do people react in these times of crisis? Some are unable to do anything because the problems overwhelm and paralyze them. These people feel insignificant. Others allow God to use those difficult circumstances as opportunities to strengthen their faith and to shape them in His image.

God gives us the choice. We can accept His help, or we can remain on the ground—shattered, hopeless, purposeless. The decision is ours.

The stained glass windows of cathedrals are examples of what can be done with glass fragments. The next time you are in a church, look carefully at the windows. Watch as the sun pierces through each colorful piece. Notice how many shapes and sizes are necessary to form the whole.

For the picture to be complete, each segment depends on every other segment.

Each pane is unique just as each of us is created by God to be totally unique. He desires to pick up the slivers which represent our lives. He mends and reshapes us in such a way that He allows more light to shine through our lives, making us whole and usable for His purposes.

God's method of reaching individuals is through other people—just ordinary people, interconnecting with one another. In the same way that the artisan carefully places each piece of glass in its perfect location, so God chooses and artistically blends all of our lives together, placing each piece of glass in the perfect location He has chosen as He fashions *His own magnificent stained glass window.* Perhaps you are the missing piece for which God has been waiting. — S.T.O.

"The body is a unit, though it is made up of many parts; and though all its parts are many, they form one body."
1 CORINTHIANS 12:12

Dear Lord,
please take the shattered pieces of my life and make me
whole. Shape me to be whom and what You desire,
and then place me in Your chosen location.
Allow Your light to shine through me. Amen.

✳

A Surprise Letter

She'll wish there was more,
and that's the great art o' letter-writin'.
CHARLES DICKENS

How can my boys relate to a man if God doesn't bring one into our lives? Jeri mused to herself. *I can't be a father as well as a mother.*

Jeri stared into the mirror. Father's Day was coming. She wished her boys had a daddy who could do all the "father" things with them. *The best I can do is be the best mom I can and pray God brings a man into our lives before they are grown up.*

Jeri taught her sons what she could, but she recognized her lack of expertise regarding a father's knowledge and know-how.

When Father's Day arrived, her sons, aged ten and twelve, kept her out of the kitchen while they fixed breakfast. When she was finally allowed to enter, she found a large card at her place. She looked at her boys, who were both smiling mischievously.

"OK, you guys. What is this all about?" she asked.

They looked at each other and giggled. "Open it, Mom."

Jeri could hardly believe what she read:

Dear Mom:

They don't make Father's Day cards for single moms, and we know you're not really our dad, Mom, but in so many ways you are. We just want to say thanks for all the "dad things" you've done for us and with us.

Thanks, Mom, for:

Teaching us to clean up our rooms because women aren't interested in sloppy men.

Allowing the belching contests we boys need to display our fledgling manhood. Thanks for letting us win sometimes!

Taking in stride all our broken bones, cuts, scrapes, and emergencies without fainting or throwing up.

Teaching us about the birds and the bees when nobody else wanted to—and for ignoring the looks we gave you for weeks afterwards.

Teaching us how to pump gas and check the oil. You let us know that cars work best when a "man" takes care of them.

Teaching us to read a map the way a man does and then to fold it back up like a woman does, so it's neat.

Showing us, when there wasn't much money, that we can use our imaginations.

Being an example of a good worker who provides for her family.

Teaching us, as much as you can, how to be men when we grow up.

Especially for teaching us to trust in Jesus.

And, Mom, in spite of what happened to you, thanks for teaching us that marriage is good, and that a father is to be honored.

We honor you, Mom. Happy Father's Day.

Love, Your Sons.

Often we feel we have to be both mother and father, but it isn't possible. God placed each of us where He desires, and He will honor us as we fulfill the duties of that position. If we have to reach outside of our own role to help our children, God watches over us with fatherly concern and helps us. — L.M.

"My son, . . . do not forsake the teaching
of your mother."
PROVERBS 6:20, NASB

Lord,
teach us to be what You called us to be. Help us to be faithful
in carrying out our responsibilities in that role and then leave
the results to You. Amen.

*

A Song of Joy

Though I know not what awaits me—
What the future has in store,
Yet, I know that God is faithful,
For I've proved Him oft before.
AUTHOR UNKNOWN

My friend, Lynn, sings solos at our church. To listen to her melodious voice, you would never suspect that she has a chronic health problem, but Lynn suffers from multiple sclerosis.

She told me, "When I found out I had MS, I was devastated. It was not a situation I expected to find myself in. Then when I lost mobility in my legs, I became depressed. I was afraid my singing ministry and my teaching would come to an end. I feared that God would not be able to use me anymore."

"I felt much the same way when I went through my divorce, Lynn," I confided. "I was afraid that my writing ministry would come to an end. Until that time, it never entered my mind that I might have to make a living as a free-lance writer and editor."

"What were your major concerns, Susan, when you made the decision to divorce?" Lynn asked.

"I thought I would starve to death," I said. "On a more serious note, I feared losing my house. Also, I was afraid there wouldn't be finances for the boys and myself to continue going to college."

Lynn smiled. "You don't look like you are malnourished."

We looked at each other and laughed. How wrong we had both been. We spent time worrying about all the things that might happen in the future instead of just dealing with today.

Lynn continued, "Finances weren't my main worry. My husband makes a good living, but I wanted to feel productive. I wanted to use my musical ability to glorify God."

"Actually none of my major fears ever came true either," I confessed. "Of course, there have often been problems and obstacles to overcome, but nothing as serious as the thoughts I conjured up in my mind before my divorce."

Lynn thought for a moment, then said, "Although I'm not where I want to be, I realize I don't have to wait until I'm there for God to use me. My voice hasn't been affected by the MS. I can still sing, and I can still teach. I just need to pace myself."

I studied my brave friend for a moment and thought about the ministry she has in our church. "I think you are more of an inspiration to others because of the obstacles you have overcome. God doesn't throw obstacles in our path for us to stumble. He wants us to glorify Him in the trials we go through. He walks with us each step of the way."

Lynn nodded in agreement. "That's true, and often the future seems so uncertain. Our security is not in our circumstances, nor in our location, but in the reality of

Jesus Christ. We discover this reality when we center our lives around the Word of God."

The next time Lynn sang at church, I noticed what an effort it was for her to walk to the platform. Yet, within the next fleeting moments, her beautiful voice removed my eyes from the difficulty I had seen and lifted them heavenward. — S.T.O.

"So we fix our eyes not on what is seen,
but on what is unseen. For what is seen is temporary,
but what is unseen is eternal."
2 CORINTHIANS 4:18

Dear Lord,
help me to keep my eyes focused on You. Use me where I am,
not where I want to be. In Jesus' name, Amen.

✳

Sweet Fragrance

Some flowers . . . must be crushed
before their full fragrance is released.
J. SIDLOW BAXTER

Poof! The fragrance of perfume filled the air. Jo put her arm across her face. "No more! I've had enough. I'll never get the smell of all these perfumes off me before the party tonight."

Teresa laughed. "I think it's fun to try out different perfumes. Each one has its own fragrance."

"Not so many at one time. It's hard to tell one from another when you do that," Jo retorted.

"Which of these is your favorite?" the saleslady asked, waving her arm toward the large array of fancy bottles. Designer labels from Elizabeth Taylor, Estée Lauder,

Oscar de la Renta, and Giorgio stood out among the lesser known fragrance designers.

"All of them!" Teresa answered. "I love perfume."

Jo pulled a tissue out of her purse and began wiping her arm. "A few of these don't blend together too well, but most of them are nice individually. Where did the idea of perfume come from, anyway?" she asked.

The saleslady commented, "I think perfume has been with us a long time. Didn't it come from Egypt—like in Cleopatra's day? I'm sure she must have used lots of it."

"We talked about fragrances in church a couple weeks ago. Remember, Teresa?" Jo asked her friend. "The use of perfume went back into ancient biblical times."

Teresa nodded her head. "Yes. They crushed lots of sweet spices together to get the best aromas. Some perfumes were used for anointing people. In fact, Jesus was anointed three times with nard, which apparently was precious in His day, and very expensive."

The two women left the department store perfume counter. Jo turned to Teresa and said, "You know, Teresa, Paul gave us that verse that says God exhibits through *us* the sweet aroma of His Son, Jesus."

"That is a beautiful thought," Teresa said. "We become the fragrance of Christ to God. Imagine that. And that fragrance can drift out to everyone, drawing them to Jesus."

"One of the things that impressed me was the necessity of the spices being crushed together before they were usable," Jo added. "Roses have to be crushed to release their scent. That made me stop and think about our lives, if we are the fragrance of Christ. We need to be crushed and broken, too."

"Yes," Teresa responded. "That way we can be blended into the sweet aroma of Christ's presence within us and become a fragrant offering to God. That's exciting."

When we see or hear perfume advertisements, we can remember that we are precious to God. He is delighted when we joyfully become the sweet fragrance of Jesus, His Beloved Son. — L.M.

> "Live a life of love,
> just as Christ loved us and gave himself up for us
> as a fragrant offering and sacrifice to God."
> EPHESIANS 5:2

Father,
what a glorious privilege You have given us. As we allow our
lives to be crushed and broken under Your hand, they release
the sweet aroma of Your Son and attract others to Him.
Thank You. Amen.

*

Picking Flowers or Weeds

CHAPTER SIX

Now it is time, through God's guidance, to make healthy, lasting decisions. There will be some gloomy days, but we can overcome them. As we begin to date, we need to be selective. If we listen with our eyes as well as our ears, we will enjoy the special moments each day brings. God provides for us as we pray and trust Him. Sometimes this requires our waiting patiently until God works out His plan for our lives in a way that strengthens and matures our faith.

✳

He Won't Let Go of Mama

Our cruel and unrelenting enemy leaves us only the choice of brave resistance, or the most abject submission.

GEORGE WASHINGTON

Melinda met Bill in college, and they immediately fell in love. They planned to marry as soon as they finished their education.

Looking back, Melinda realizes she should have recognized the warning signs. "Whenever we wanted to do something, Bill consulted his mother first. I put up with it because I thought once we were married, things would be different. Then, we would make our own decisions. Boy! Was I wrong." She shook her head and let out a loud sigh.

"His mother even planned our wedding. My suggestions were ignored. I resented her more and more, but I was biding my time until we had our own apartment."

"Did it work out?" I asked.

"No! Bill continued to confer with her about everything. He allowed her to have the final say in every aspect of our lives. It was hard to accept. I became tense and stressed out.

"I took good care of Bill by fixing nourishing meals. I kept the house clean, ironed his clothes, and worked hard to make our marriage a success. His mother didn't care. She continually criticized me until I felt I couldn't do anything right. Life was miserable."

"Couldn't you talk to Bill?" I questioned. "Did he realize what she was doing?"

"I tried to talk to him, but he was so used to her making his decisions, he expected it. When she wasn't around, he agreed with me, but when she was there, he did what she wanted. The situation was frustrating."

"How long were you married?" I asked.

"For over twelve years. I can't believe I allowed it to go on that long," she answered. "We didn't have any children for several years, because dear Mama controlled even that. 'Later,' she would tell Bill, 'when you're more established.' I hoped having a child would help Bill grow up, but it didn't.

"At least it was *my* decision to get a divorce." She smiled. "It was one thing Mama didn't decide, although she was happy about it. She wanted Bill all to herself."

"That sounds sick," I said. "Did she have other children?"

"Yes, all sons," Melinda said. "Guess what! They all live with her, including Bill. She keeps them totally dependent. She rules over them the way she did Bill. It's sad."

"Mama's boys" are not capable of having independent relationships with their wives. Unless the apron strings are broken, there is no chance of a healthy marriage.

Melinda is now her own person, making her own choices. The decisions she makes, with God's help, are the right ones for her and her daughter. Her stress and nervousness have disappeared, and she has found meaningful relationships with friends. She looks forward to her future.

It's hard to cope when someone else makes your decisions and ignores your needs or wishes. There are times when you must search out God's will, take a stand, and hold firmly to it. — L.M.

"Be strong in the Lord, and in His mighty power."
EPHESIANS 6:10

Father,
help me to be strong and wrest myself from another's determination to rule my life. I need Your wisdom to make healthful choices and stick to them. Thank You. Amen.

✳

The Fire

Faith can place a candle in the darkest night.
AUTHOR UNKNOWN

Mom, I had to abandon my car," my son's voice sounded desperate and breathless on the other end of the telephone line. "Flames were jumping across the highway. Burning branches fell into the back of my convertible."

"Are you OK?" I asked, concern filling my voice.

"Oh, Mom, I'm fine, but I'm worried about what might happen to my car."

"Tell me what happened. Maybe I can help," I offered.

"I was on my way home from class, and I could see the fire burning out of control in the Santa Barbara hills, but then it seemed like it was still far away. The freeway was blocked, so I took the old highway towards town.

"About halfway there, everyone on both sides of the road had been told to evacuate their homes. People were all trying to leave at the same time, and there was a huge traffic jam. Suddenly, flames jumped across the highway, and that's when it happened."

Rich was talking so fast that I didn't understand everything. "That's when what happened?" I asked.

"My clutch cable snapped, and I couldn't shift gears. I pulled to the side of the road and had to abandon my car."

"What did you do then?"

"I called my girlfriend to come get me. Mom, I can't afford to lose my car. I don't have comprehensive insurance on it, and I'll have to drop out for a semester if I can't get to school."

I knew Rich was right. Rich's finances for his college education were extremely tight. Without his car, he'd have to leave school and obtain a full-time job to earn money for a new one. I saw no alternative.

"Let's pray about it, Rich. God knows the situation."

I rarely pray for material possessions, and I've never prayed for a car before, but this time I did. "Lord, You know Rich needs that beat-up Volvo convertible to get to his college classes. Please spare it in this fire. We pray that the fire will soon be contained."

Three days later, I received another call from Rich. "Mom, they finally let me check on my car. I caught a ride back to where I left it. The fire burned to within a hundred feet, and it's full of ashes, but it runs. It's in the shop now getting a new clutch cable."

God teaches us to pray specifically. He knew that car was important to Rich's education, so He spared it. With what took place, I learned an important lesson: When things look bleakest, God is there, showing His presence in the smallest details of our lives. — S.T.O.

"You do not have, because you do not ask God."
JAMES 4:2

Lord,
thank You for hearing our prayers. Thank You for caring
about even the smallest details of our lives. Amen.

✳

How Do I Find Love?

When we are unable to find tranquillity within ourselves,
it is useless to seek it elsewhere.
LA ROCHEFOUCAULD

Oh, Lori," I said in exasperation. "Another man?"

Lori hung her head for a moment, then looked at me woefully. "I can't seem to change my behavior. I chase after every man who looks at me. I think he must be interested or he wouldn't pay attention to me. I do it over and over."

"It's hard to learn from our mistakes," I said.

"There have been so many men. Although I have expectations, the men never intend to get involved, so I move on to the next one."

"You went through therapy, didn't you?" I asked.

"Yes, but I wasn't really listening. I was too anxious for someone to care about me and provide me with self-worth for the therapy to do any good."

"How about your friend John? God used him in your life."

"Yes. God used John to help me realize I could have a relationship without getting serious. Yet, after he died, I looked for other men to fill the hole he left.

"I attended a retreat. One man paid twenty dollars for me to go horseback riding. I was excited—someone thought I was worthwhile to pay that much money. We prayed and went to Bible studies together. I thought, *This must be the one.* How many times I'd thought that.

"One night he didn't talk with me or join the prayer group. I realized he had only wanted to be friends."

"Lori, until you become satisfied within yourself with who you are, you'll never find the right man," I stated.

"You're right. I have such a focus on guys instead of the Lord. I'm attracted to the wrong types of men, and I pick men who are basically unavailable. For instance, I met Tom, who is different. We talked for hours and hours on the phone. Things seemed to be moving along with him, so I confronted him with our relationship. I told him I loved him. He looked at me so pained. He was only looking for a friendship. He wanted a woman closer to his own age, since he is a lot younger. It hurt to hear that."

"Lori, you have a pattern going."

"I realize that, and I want to break it. What can I do?" she asked.

"You should stop trying to settle for second best and wait until God brings the right person into your life," I stated. "As you let go of wrong relationships and seek God's will, you are going to be restored to wholeness. Then you can become a gift to the man God has for you. You become his jewel. You need to remember that."

Lori is finally realizing she doesn't need to continue her unsuitable behavior. God will bring the man who will know she is a gift from Him and will treasure her. She is becoming satisfied with who she is. Are you? — L.M.

"[Let your adorning] be the hidden person of the heart with the imperishable jewel of a gentle and quiet spirit, which in God's sight is very precious."
1 Peter 3:4, rsv

Father,
sometimes I forget that I am precious in Your sight. Teach me
to be satisfied with the jewel You are designing me to be. I
rest myself in Your hand. Amen.

✳

106

Listen with Your Eyes

God is eager to teach us through almost every event in our lives if we are but willing to listen.

Tim Hansel

Running into the kitchen, my son chattered on and on as he held the bird feeder he was building with the help of his older brother. "Look, Mommy. See the little perches? I sanded them smooth so the birds won't hurt their feet," Mike said excitedly.

Up to my elbows in dough, kneading it as he spoke, I said, "Uh-huh." Mentally I was reviewing the dinner menu, checking off each item to make sure everything would be ready at the same time.

Mike continued his chatter. "I wonder what kind of birds will come and eat? The bird house is almost finished. Let's go buy some birdseed tomorrow. Doesn't it look great?"

Every few minutes I said, "Uh-huh," to show Mike I was listening, but my thoughts were far away.

"What color should I paint it, Mommy?" Mike asked. When he received no reply, he suggested, "Red, or maybe blue, or maybe white with brown trim like our house? What do you think, Mommy?"

Glancing at the clock, I realized that my dinner guests would arrive in half an hour. The bread wouldn't be ready. I wasn't dressed and hadn't even thought about what I would wear. As my mind whirled with these thoughts, I almost totally ignored my son.

"Where should we hang it, Mommy? On the tree? On the patio? Where, Mommy? Huh? Mommy, are you listening?" Suddenly Mike's pleading tone caught my attention. I looked down into his huge blue eyes, brimming with tears.

"Mommy, I want you to listen to me," he begged.

"I am, dear," I replied as I folded the dough into a pan.

"No, Mommy. You're not listening. You're not listening with your eyes," Mike said softly.

Suddenly I realized what my son meant. More importantly, I knew he was right. I placed the dough in the oven and washed my hands. Then I bent down and hugged him. "Now I'm listening with my ears *and* my eyes. Why don't you paint the birdhouse white with brown trim so it will match our house? There's some leftover paint in the shed. I'll show you where it is before I dress."

The dinner guests could wait. — S.T.O.

"I love the Lord because he hears my prayers and
answers them. Because he bends down and listens, I
will pray as long as I breathe!"
PSALM 116:1–2, TLB

Dear Lord,
teach us to listen with our eyes as well as our ears. Help us
not to crowd out the special moments of each day. Amen.

*

Let God Do His Thing

Faith is . . . to believe the things which we cannot see and
cannot understand and cannot fathom.
M. R. DeHaan

Send out your applications right away, Thelma, to any recommended agricultural schools," I told my daughter. "The sooner you have them in the mail, the better chance you have of being accepted."

Thelma sent out several applications and was accepted at California Polytechnic University, San Luis Obispo. We were both delighted. She applied for grants from the State of California and received help for her first year. My savings provided the remaining amount. When I received the tuition bill for Thelma's second year, she was still eligible for a couple of grants, but an additional twelve hundred dollars was needed.

This large sum loomed as impossible. We had no solution, so we gave our problem to the Lord and left the decision with Him. If Thelma was to continue in college, God would have to meet this need, because we did not have the money. Strangely, we had peace of mind and did not worry. We placed complete confidence in God.

About two weeks before the tuition deadline, I received a surprise phone call from some friends who owned a small business. A few years prior, I had invested one thousand dollars in their partnership. Since they had made no profit, no dividends had been paid. Through the years, I had almost forgotten about it.

"We have decided that we are going to terminate our partnership and incorporate instead," the owner told me. "Even though we haven't made any profit, we feel we owe you a little extra for our use of your money, so we are mailing you a check for twelve hundred dollars."

When I informed Thelma, we laughed joyously and praised the Lord for His provision. What a marvelous witness this was! God knows in advance what we will be facing, and He goes before us to make a way. Since that day, we both have had confidence that our Heavenly Father will be faithful when other seemingly impossible situations arise. Over the years, that has proven true.

Sometimes we have to wait for a solution while our faith is severely tested. I think the answer lies in being totally submitted to Him, without becoming anxious. We need to wait patiently until He works out His plan for our lives in ways that strengthen and mature our faith. — LM.

"And my God shall supply all your needs according to His riches in glory in Christ Jesus."
PHILIPPIANS 4:19, NASB

Dear God,
what a wonderful Father You are! Thank You for always being there when we are incapable of meeting our own needs. We gratefully acknowledge Your faithfulness. Amen.

*

A Gentle Attitude

The greatest gift you can give another
is to allow him to be himself.
AUTHOR UNKNOWN

The front door was slammed angrily. My son stomped down the stairs and out of earshot. Only silence remained.

Why do I fight with my son? My stomach churned. I had planned what to say, but when he stood there, hands on his hips, looking so defiant . . .

I stared out the window, watching his tall, lanky form disappear down the street. When he was young, he usually obeyed me. I could answer his questions. We agreed on most issues.

Now that he'd become a teenager, I didn't have pat answers. Plus, I no longer had a spouse to confer with or to discuss the problems that seemed to arise daily as my son struggled to find his own identity.

Overwhelmed with emotion, I sank onto the couch and buried my face in my hands. Raising a son alone was almost more responsibility than I could handle. Even when I carefully planned my words in advance, my emotions took over as soon as I opened my mouth. I'd read books by Christian psychologists on how to deal with teens, but the words seemed useless when I tried them out in real life. Why couldn't I find a rule book with all the answers?

My eyes strayed to my closed Bible, lying on the coffee table. I couldn't remember the last time I had opened it. In years past, I had faithfully spent time with God in His Word. Since my world had been turned upside down, I'd neglected God as well as myself and my son.

Hesitantly, I opened my Bible to the Proverbs. As I began to read, the invisible weight on my shoulders began to evaporate. I prayed, not for material things or a change in circumstances, but for wisdom in dealing with my son.

The realization came to me that my child was growing up and that my role in his life was changing. My answers weren't enough anymore. He needed to explore his own way, to find his own explanations to life's questions.

My job was to love and support him. We might not always agree, but we could try to understand each other. This would require work on my part. When I disagreed with him, I needed to listen to his point of view. Talking openly with him, but not pushing my own ideas, was vital. Also, I needed to admit that I don't have all the answers.

The front door opened and slammed shut. I looked up at the tall, young man who waited for my response.

"I've been thinking while you were gone, and I'm beginning to see your point of view," I said. "I don't necessarily agree with you, but I think I understand how you feel, and I respect your opinion."

I stood up and hugged my son.

He returned my embrace and softly said, "Thanks, Mom." — S.T.O.

"A gentle answer turns away wrath,
but a harsh word stirs up anger."
PROVERBS 15:1

Dear God,
help me to open my mind to the viewpoints of others,
especially my son. Teach me to be understanding and
compassionate. Amen.

✳

Finding Strength

In the darkest day, we can still hope . . .
in the unconquerable power of God.
WILLIAM BARCLAY

I've had it!" Sylvia yelled at her husband. "You have done nothing to keep our marriage together. I've tried until I'm sick and tired of trying."

"What have *you* done?" her husband demanded sarcastically.

"I have gone to Lion-Tamers and New Hope at church for *five years* so to help me understand why you drink so much and why both of our families have alcoholic backgrounds. You have refused to go to counseling with me. You won't participate in anything to help our family or yourself.

"I've done everything I know how to do to keep our marriage together. I've had it with your rages of anger and your drinking binges. You've changed so much that I don't know you anymore."

"Well, that's just too bad, isn't it!" he sneered at her.

"I'm not the only one," Sylvia retorted. "Our daughter hates it when you're in one of your stupors. You are going to lose her love completely if you don't do something about your drinking."

Sylvia's husband glared at her at the mention of their daughter, Crystal. "I'd do anything for her. I love her!"

"Then why don't you show her? The only way she sees you now is with a drink in your hand. Your eyes become bleary, and you slur your words. Plus you smell like a brewery. It's disgusting. Crystal doesn't even want to be around you anymore, and neither do I. I've decided to divorce you," Sylvia stated.

She then filed for separation, and a year-and-a-half later she and her husband were divorced.

Crystal was torn between her parents, feeling she had to choose which one she loved the most. Her school grades went down, and her self-esteem declined. Sylvia took her daughter in for counseling. In time Crystal came to realize she didn't have to choose between her parents. They both loved her. Today, at nine years of age, she still grieves over the divorce, but she is making adjustments to her young life.

After her divorce, Sylvia began attending our single-parent group at church. She has learned to build new relationships with the opposite sex which do not involve physical intimacy. Instead, she has discovered the close-ness found in friendship and faith.

"God is helping me adjust to my new life," she told me. "I'm building a safe place for Crystal and myself. I'm making friends with people who desire to build healthy relationships with each other and with God. I'm reaching out in ways I never did before and depending totally on God. He is my support, my confidante, and the One who guides me. He has become my life. Walking with Him daily, I know I'm going to make it," she smiled confidently.

"The divorce has been hard. But it becomes easier as I grow more aware of God's constant presence and experience His guidance and support. I'm walking victoriously through each day as I look to Him." — L.M.

> "I can do all things through Him [Christ] who strengthens me."
> PHILIPPIANS 4:13, NASB

Father,
you give me assurance to conquer every ordeal I meet because
I am strengthened by Your love and presence through the
Christian friends You bring into my life. Amen.

✳

"I'll Be Here for You"

The only gift is a portion of thyself.
AUTHOR UNKNOWN

The telephone rang, and my twenty-three-year-old son said, "Mom, I'm so glad you're home. I need to talk to you. Laura tried to commit suicide last night, but I stopped her."

"Rich, do you want me to stop by your place on the way to work? I'd be happy to."

He replied, "No, that's OK. I just want to talk awhile."

"Take all the time you need," I told him. "Tell me what happened."

A few months earlier, Rich had helped his friend, Laura, through a difficult time in her life. He encouraged her to see a psychologist for her depression and drug problem. He thought she was doing much better—until last night.

Rich continued, "Laura left a message on my voice mail. I had checked my messages fifteen minutes earlier, but a small inner voice told me to check them again."

"You know who that was, don't you?" I asked, never missing an opportunity to witness to my jet-setting son who rarely took time to go to church.

"Oh, Mom, I know you pray for me all the time. You've told me you pray that angels will surround me and protect me." He added softly, "I guess this time they really did. If she had died, I would have felt so guilty and would have wondered if I could have done more for her. All my life, I would have carried that burden."

"Thankfully, you stopped her. Now tell me what happened."

Rich continued, "I checked my messages the second time, and there was one new one—from Laura. Her voice sounded groggy, distant. I knew something was terribly wrong. I told my roommate, and we rushed to her house. Later we found out she had taken an overdose of pain killers, downed a bottle of wine, and taken some other drugs."

I interrupted my son, "Is she going to be all right?"

"The doctor said she would have died if we had not found her when we did. I'm so thankful I checked my answering machine a second time. I rarely do that."

We talked for about an hour—about dealing with the situation, what he could do, and what he needed to leave in God's hands. Finally, Rich said, "Mom, I'm glad I caught you before you left. It helps to know you're there."

"I'll always be here for you—no matter what. Why don't you stop by for dinner one night next week?"

I hung up the telephone and reflected on the situation. When our children are grown and leading their own lives, it's easy to think our jobs as parents are done. Yet, the older they are, the more serious their problems become. It is so important to keep the channels of communication open.

When my son needs me, I can always rearrange my work schedule for him. He is far more important than any of my job-oriented tasks. Plus, I can pray for him and for Laura, too. I pray that God will make His presence known to her in a real and personal way so that she no longer feels a craving for alcohol or drugs. We never know the far-reaching effect of our intercessory prayers. — S.T.O.

"For now is the time—you are bending down to hear! You are ready with a plentiful supply of love and kindness. Now answer my prayer and rescue me as you promised."

PSALM 69:13, TLB

Lord,
thank You for always being here for us. Help us to follow Your example and to be available always for our children, whatever their ages. In Jesus' name, Amen.

✳

The Price of Freedom

CHAPTER SEVEN

There is always a price attached to freedom. When we make wrong choices, there are consequences which may result in trials. Sometimes we are imprisoned by our bitterness and lack of forgiveness. Freedom also means letting go of our children as they grow up and take responsibility for their own lives. With God's help, we can break free of our chains and become independent.

✳

A Fork in the Road

When I stepped out in faith and allowed you to lead, Lord,
you provided more than I hoped for.

AUTHOR UNKNOWN

I gripped my son's hand tightly as we hiked along the path through the towering redwoods. The massive trees shut out most of the sunlight. A light fog made the trail visible for only a few feet in front of us.

Suddenly, we came to a fork in the road. Mike's trusting eyes looked up at me as he asked, "Which way do we go, Mom?" He didn't know that I possessed no natural sense of direction. He assumed I knew the way out of the woods, but I had become caught up in listening to him and hadn't paid attention to where we had walked.

I paused for a moment before making a decision. The thought came to me of how often we reach forks in our lives. Frequently, I have drawn hasty conclusions that have affected my entire life. How different my experience would have been if I had chosen the other direction.

Other times, I have agonized for years, searching for the correct solution. One of the hardest decisions I ever made was to divorce my husband of twenty-two years. It was not easy. I could not see clearly down that path, either. Yet, at the time, I felt it was necessary for the well-being of myself and my sons.

Choices have consequences. Often they require us to release the familiar and to venture into the unknown. Resolutions involve taking risks. We need to be willing to change and to grow.

Yet, our decisions, whether large or small, should not be made alone. God wants us to consult Him for even the smallest incidents. Through prayer and reading His Word, we are able to stay in His will. With His help, we will make the right choices at every fork.

I bowed my head and silently asked God to help me make the right choice. I looked down one fork of the trail dividing the world's tallest trees and saw only redwoods surrounded by fog. When I strained my eyes to see down the other fork, I saw a faint amber light in the distance, which I recognized as the sign on top of the mountain cabin resort where we were staying. With confidence I said, "This is the right path, Mike. Let's go." — S.T.O.

"Show me the path where I should go, O Lord; point out the right road for me to walk."
PSALM 25:4, TLB

Dear Lord,
guide me as I reach each fork on my journey of life. Help me
to make the right choices along the way. Amen.

✳

Watch for Red Lights

The closer we walk with God, the clearer we see His guidance.
AUTHOR UNKNOWN

When Debbie prays specifically, she often sees red or green lights in her mind. She prayed before marrying Andy, and red lights flashed everywhere. However, she loved him, so she ignored the red lights and went ahead with the marriage.

Debbie wanted God's answer only if it coincided with her wishes. She later regretted her action. Their marriage was rocky, almost from the start.

A while later, Debbie's best friend, Sabrina, needed a place to stay. Debbie's husband insisted that she stay with them. Sabrina was only to stay a short time, but six months later she was still with them. Then, Debbie found out Sabrina and her husband had been sleeping together.

"I don't believe this!" Debbie was livid with anger and hurt. "You're having an affair with my best friend right here in our home? How could you? She's only staying here because you insisted on it, and now this?"

Her husband promised to behave, so Sabrina stayed with them, even though she knew Debbie didn't want her there. Then Debbie found out that the affair was continuing. That left no alternative—Sabrina *had* to leave.

For the next six months, Debbie kept asking herself what she would do if the marriage broke up. What were her options? She realized, thinking back, that she never should have married Andy, but he kept promising to behave. She should have paid attention to the red lights.

They began having terrible fights, along with emotional manipulation and hurt. Even so, Debbie *still* wanted to make her marriage work. She talked with her husband, and he assured her he wouldn't see Sabrina again. However, less than two weeks later, he was with her.

That was the last straw. When Debbie confronted him, he admitted it. She told him, "You wanted a separation. Well, you've got one now."

Debbie has gone through some hard trials because she thought she could ignore God's "red light." Many times we cause our own misery by doing what we want to do, rather than listening to God. Now, when Debbie faces a trial, she prays and asks the Lord what He wants her to learn. She pays strict attention to any red lights.

Our loving Father gives us indications of His will in our hearts and minds. We're free to do what we want, but often we suffer consequences as a result. His desire is that we accept His will. As Debbie stated so emphatically, "Pay attention to those red lights." — L.M.

"Let the wise listen and add to their learning, and let the discerning get guidance."
PROVERBS 1:5

Lord,
teach me to heed the warnings You give me so that when I am tested, I will endure in the strength my faith produces, and I will rest in Your freedom. Amen.

✳

Forget and Forgive

He who cannot forgive others
breaks the bridge over which he himself must pass.
AUTHOR UNKNOWN

When I walked into my Single Parent Fellowship meeting, I saw Vivian seated in the corner. Her glance caught mine, and she brushed a wisp of long, chestnut hair out of her eyes. Vivian stared at me a moment, as though waiting for my reaction to seeing her again.

Although months had passed since our paths last crossed, it seemed like yesterday. I thought that I had forgiven her, but the old familiar feelings of resentment and anger welled up inside of me. She had wronged me. Yet, she never said she was sorry, nor had she asked for my forgiveness.

All these thoughts raced through my mind, but no amount of rationalization could take away the churning in my stomach. I wanted to rush up, shake her, and shout, "Why aren't you sorry?" Instead, I just stared back at her.

To my surprise, Vivian stood up and walked towards me. I closed my eyes and said a silent prayer. *Lord, help me deal with this unexpected situation. Help me react in the way You desire.*

In that brief moment, God softened my heart. Seeing Vivian once again made me realize that I had never truly forgiven her. I had shoved my emotions below the surface so I wouldn't have to deal with the bitterness and hurt.

When I opened my eyes and she stood beside me, I was able to picture her in a different light. Now, she looked vulnerable, unsure. Had I overreacted before because of my hurt?

After an awkward silence, I smiled and said, "It's been a long time. I'm glad you came tonight." As I spoke, I genuinely meant those words. The built-up resentment and anger had vanished with my prayer.

She lowered her head and stammered, "I wasn't sure you'd want to see me again."

Pondering her words, I stared at the lock of her hair which had fallen down again. I realized that the next move needed to be mine. "Let's forget the past," I offered, waiting for her response. She nodded her head, unconsciously brushing the chestnut wisp back in place again.

"The refreshments are over there." I pointed to the corner. "Are you thirsty?"

"Yes," she answered.

Wanting to reach beyond the small talk, I remembered that someone had told me Vivian's mother had been in a serious car accident six months ago. "How is your mother doing? I heard about her accident."

She looked relieved. For the first time, her body seemed to relax, and a slight smile formed on her lips. "Mother's doing much better," she answered. "She's been staying with me during her rehabilitation." She paused for a moment, then said softly, "Thank you for asking."

As we walked toward the refreshment table together, I realized that my lack of forgiveness had cost us both a great price. — S.T.O.

> "Be kind and compassionate to one another, forgiving each other, just as in Christ God forgave you."
> EPHESIANS 4:32

Dear Lord,
please help me not to allow resentment to build in my heart.
Teach me to forgive and forget. Amen.

*

Rebekah

There is in every true woman's heart a spark of heavenly fire . . . which kindles up, and beams and blazes in the dark hour of adversity.
WASHINGTON IRVING

I may *never* have any grandchildren," I lamented. "I don't think my daughter will ever get married."

Sitting across the table at a Sunday brunch, my friend Iris said, "Well, if you want to adopt a grandchild, I have a daughter who doesn't have any grandparents near. She would enjoy having you as a 'grandmother.'"

Rebekah, her daughter, and I looked at each other and laughed. She was a lovely, sixteen-year-old girl.

"How about it, Rebekah, would you like that?" I asked.

"It might be fun," she replied.

From then on, I became her "local" grandmother.

Rebekah was a member of the high school track team. Cross-country running was her favorite event. She was also involved in her youth group at church and deeply loved her Lord.

We enjoyed our grandmother-granddaughter relationship for about a year-and-a-half.

Then, on the Wednesday before Easter, my phone rang. It was Iris. "I just came home and found Rebekah covered with bruises. She has *not* fallen or been in an accident, so we know something is very wrong. I'm taking her to the hospital right away. Please pray for her."

"Of course," I said. "Beginning right now!"

The doctors found that Rebekah had developed a rare, fast-acting form of leukemia. She hemorrhaged inside, which caused the bruises. Her last words were, "I didn't know . . . was so much fun!" Iris didn't catch the word, but because of the expression on Rebekah's face, she assumed it was either "Jesus" or "heaven." Rebekah went into a coma and shortly afterwards was pronounced brain-dead.

Iris had to make the heart-breaking decision to take her daughter off life support systems—on Good Friday.

Later, I received a lovely note from Iris: "Thank you so much for loving my princess. You have given me the greatest gift a mother can receive."

How do we cope with circumstances like this? Iris relied totally on God's strength and grace to pull her through the difficult weeks following Rebekah's physical death. She knows Rebekah is running through the green fields of heaven with a perfect body, laughing and filled with joy as she delights in the love and presence of her Savior.

Even so, Iris's world is shattered! There is now no one to come home to, to share her joys or sorrows—no one to take on a shopping spree for clothes, to talk about school or dreams and hopes for the future.

Losing a loved one through death is one of life's most difficult experiences. Only when we stay close to Jesus, our Lord, can we find the courage to live through the agonies and face the future. He has the answers for each painful event in our lives, and He alone provides the stability and peace we need. — L.M.

"The sufferings of this present time are not worthy to be compared with the glory that is to be revealed to us."
ROMANS 8:18, NASB

Father,
hold us tightly when death takes a loved one. Ease our
sorrow. Wipe away our tears. Teach us to face the future
alone by trusting You. In Jesus' name, Amen.

✳

Slow Me Down, Lord

True wisdom lies in gathering precious moments
out of each day.
AUTHOR UNKNOWN

Waves rolled into shore, breaking a few feet from my sand chair. At last, I had captured some time for myself! I dug my toes into the warm sand and breathed the cool ocean air. It was a perfect day to watch my teenage son, Mike, and his friend, Carl, surf.

Mike caught a wave and rode it into shore. He was easy to spot on his florescent orange surfboard I had given him for his birthday. He maneuvered his agile body, stepping back and forth to keep the center of the board balanced on the crest of the wave.

The wave dissipated, and Mike effortlessly slid off. He shouted, "That was a great one, Mom. Did you see me ride it in?" I nodded. He grabbed his surfboard, tucked it under his arm, and darted back into the foaming surf.

I almost turned my son down when he asked, "Want to join Carl and me at the beach? You haven't watched me surf, Mom, since Dad . . . ahhhh, in a long time."

He was right. I hadn't gone to the beach with him since his father left. Working, coping with household chores and repairs, and just adjusting to being single again had consumed all my time. I felt exhausted and frazzled. Rushing from one activity to another, I never felt a sense of accomplishment.

The teenagers straddled their surfboards, bobbing up and down in the water. Mike misjudged a wave, stood up too soon, and ended up sliding off his board. Carl and I laughed. Mike came up spewing water and laughing, too.

It had been a long time since I relaxed and laughed like this. How good it felt to sit in my sand chair with no demands on my time.

Mike glanced back to see if I was watching him, just like he did when he was a little boy. Then he eased onto his board and captured another wave. It meant a great deal to him that I had said yes when he invited me to go along.

Were my priorities out of order? Was I always too busy "doing" to take time to "enjoy" God's gifts to me? One of the greatest gifts God had given me was my son. The day would soon come when he would no longer invite me on a beach outing. Now was my opportunity to spend time with this young man who was growing up before my eyes.

Watching another wave surge into shore, a sense of God's peace enveloped me. The tension in my neck and back muscles began to ease. For the first time in months, I stopped worrying about all the undone chores at home. Instead, I concentrated on the present moment and the special time I was able to spend with Mike.

Just as Mike waited to be lifted up on the crest of the right wave, we, too, need to pause to catch God's words when He speaks. His voice is often soft like a whisper. Only when we slow down to listen can He guide us according to His will. — S.T.O.

"Be still, and know that I am God."
PSALM 46:10

Dear Lord,
help me to pause and listen for Your voice. Allow Your words
to fill me with peace. Teach me to "ride the waves" of Your
will for my life. Amen.

✳

Walking Away from Abuse

Too many today . . . refuse to accept anything that approaches
the sense of responsibility.
JOSEPH SIZOO

My marriage was not happy, but I never expected an abusive one," Mary Lou said tiredly. "I held on as long as I could, but things became so bad that I knew I had to end it."

"What led you to that decision?" I asked.

"My parents' home was abusive. After witnessing the drinking, arguments, and fighting between my parents, I married to get away. Things were all right for about seven years. Then my husband began to change. *He* became abusive—just like my parents.

"We had two daughters by then, and I was determined our home would not be like my parents' home. At first, I wouldn't let him yell or fight in front of the girls. I tried to shield them. However, the fighting became worse.

"In our seventh year, I had major surgery. I wanted him to be understanding, but he wasn't. I was home for about a week when he tried to rape me. Then, he beat me. I knew our marriage was over. Yet, I stayed for another six years, because I kept hoping it would work."

"Why did you stay in the marriage when it took this turn?" I asked in astonishment.

"Mostly because of the money situation. We both worked, but still weren't making it financially, so I knew I would never be able to make it alone raising two girls. Even so, it became imperative for me to leave because of the abuse.

"Afterwards, I totally lost control of myself for the first five or six years. I provided a home for the girls, but I abandoned them emotionally."

"How did you lose control, Mary Lou?"

"I drank, I ate, and I formed unhealthy relationships. Finally, I realized I had to get help, because I wasn't doing myself or my girls any good. The only thing left was to cry out to God for help. God began to work in my life and show me that He had always been there for me, but He was waiting until I acknowledged my need for Him.

"Later I went to therapy. The past few years have been years of deliverance from the garbage that went on throughout my life. The therapy helped greatly, but without the Lord, recovery would not have been permanent.

"One of the important things I did was begin making some concerted efforts in changing my life and accepting responsibility. I hadn't done that before.

"Today, I try to forget the past. The Lord has drawn me close so I know who I am in Christ. He has become everything to me.

"He's also led me into leadership in the women's ministry of our single parents' group at church. Even in the midst of my struggles, through God's help, I have learned to be free from both abuse and addictions and to become responsible for my behavior. That has made all the difference." — L.M.

"It was for freedom that Christ set us free;
therefore, keep standing firm and do not be subject
again to a yoke of slavery."
GALATIANS 5:1, NASB

Father,
it is easy to allow ourselves to be abused in one way or
another. Impress on us that freedom develops as we accept our
responsibilities in serving You. Amen.

✳

The Apron Strings

There are only two lasting things we can give our children.
One is roots, the other, wings.
AUTHOR UNKNOWN

One of the most difficult times for me as a mother was allowing my oldest son to go away to college. When he graduated from high school, I wrote him the following letter:

Dear Rich,

Today is your high school graduation. I have spent the last eighteen years teaching and guiding you. Now it is time to let you go and to allow you to choose your own way.

As you were growing up, I shared your victories and defeats. I cheered at your swim meets and applauded at your cello concerts. I watched a skinny, freckle-faced blonde boy change into a handsome, six-foot-three muscular young man.

As a mother, the hardest job for me is to let go—to allow our roles to change. I worked hard at being your mother, and now I want to enjoy being your friend. As a token of my feelings and my confidence in you, I'm enclosing my apron strings in this letter. They are cut off from my apron to symbolize your total freedom.

Yet, you know that I will be only a phone call away. I want to continue to share your life, to hear about your experiences, to be there when you need me. The difference is that now you are in the driver's seat, and I'm the passenger.

I believe in you, and I love you very much. Congratulations, Son!

All my love,
Mom

As parents, we spend many years helping our children to establish firm foundations for their lives. As they grow older, we hope they will continue to build on those foundations. Finally, the time comes to hand them the hammers and nails and let them go. In this way, we allow them to lead their own lives, make their own decisions, and accept the responsibility for their own mistakes.

It is especially difficult for single mothers to cut our apron strings. Because of our loneliness and overwhelming needs, we sometimes tend to cling too tightly to our children. Yet, there is a delicate balance between maintaining a close family atmosphere and smothering our grown children.

I often look back to the day seven years ago when I wrote that letter to a high school graduate. I compare that relationship with the one I enjoy today with my twenty-six-year-old son. He has become one of my very best friends. Although his present job takes him around the world, he continues to keep in touch by telephone and postcards.

Today, no matter how many miles separate me from my firstborn, we will always be close. When he returns home for a visit, I share his adventures and his dreams as I always have and hope I always will. — S.T.O.

"Follow my advice, my son . . . Guard my words as your most precious possession. Write them down, and also keep them deep within your heart."
PROVERBS 7:2–3, TLB

Lord,
thank You, for my children—for the joy and love we share.
Help me to be a loving parent and a good friend to my grown
sons. Amen.

✳

Fettered or Free?

Courage is the price that life exacts for granting peace. The
soul that knows it not, knows no release.
AMELIA EARHART PUTNAM

How can I forgive Bob? It's too hard. He ruined my life as well as our daughter's. I don't think I'll ever be able to forgive him—and I really don't want to!" Having said that, I folded my arms and glared at my friend, June.

After a moment she said, "I feel the same way. Maybe we need to examine the meaning of forgiveness."

"I already know what forgiveness means," I snapped.

"How would you define it?" June asked.

"It means to forget about what someone did to you." I knew it was a lame answer. I picked up my Bible and turned to a familiar verse in Luke: "Jesus said, 'Forgive, and you will be forgiven.' That's all He said."

"Is there a note in the margin?" June asked.

"'Release and you will be released, set free and you will be set free.' Hmmm, I never noticed those words before. Were they always on this page?" We both laughed.

Thoughtfully, June commented, "When I forgive someone, I release him or set him free."

"Yes, that's part of it," I said excitedly, "but there is more than that. Listen to the resulting action!" I read it again slowly. "'Set free, and you will be set free.' Jesus said if I let go of my anger and bitterness toward Bob and forgive him for hurting me, I set myself free. That's why I need to forgive. I've never seen that before."

For several minutes, we both sat in silence while we thought about this new concept. Glancing at June, I said, "June, Jesus can't work effectively in our lives if we do not forgive. He wants *us* free, so He can use us. I need to forgive Bob, and you need to forgive your ex-husband, too." It was June's turn to glare at me.

Why didn't I want to forgive? As I thought about this concept, I realized that my stubborn pride and arrogance demanded that my former husband be punished. He had to pay a sufficient price for the pain I had suffered, and until that was satisfied, I wouldn't forgive him. How blind I had been!

"June, God purchased our freedom from sin at a great price to Himself and also to His Son. Jesus accepted His death on the cross. However, in my stubbornness, I couldn't forgive Bob. Instead, I wrapped chains around myself, as well as around him. By not releasing him and allowing my forgiveness to reach out to him, I prevented God's love from working, not only in Bob's life, but in my own as well."

June nodded in agreement. "Has it been worth the bitterness in our hearts, worth the anger and the stress we've felt?"

No. It had not.

Making my decision, I picked up the phone and dialed a number. A voice answered. I said, "Bob, do you have a few minutes to talk?" — L.M.

"Forgive, and you will be forgiven."
LUKE 6:37

Father God,
what damage I have caused in my own life, as well as in the
lives of others, by not heeding Your words to forgive. Help me
to be as free at forgiving another and setting us both free as
You have been toward me. Amen.

✳

Harvest Time

I've Grown Through Pain

Perfect Timing

Dormant Bulbs

The Sudden Urge

Hang in There, Baby!

The Soap Opera

Fulfilling My Dreams

Turning Frogs into Princes

CHAPTER EIGHT

Through our acceptance and growth, we reap benefits and are able to take stock of our situation. God teaches us patience and acceptance. Often what He has in mind for us is better than anything we could have imagined ourselves. Sometimes God seems to shut doors, but He opens others again when He is ready to move us forward. He is always there for us, and He will never give us more than we can endure.

✳

I've Grown Through Pain

*The children of godly parents are
the children of many prayers.*

John Bunyan

Jeri set two cups of steaming coffee on the end table and curled up on the sofa. As we talked, she brought up the subject of her divorce.

"I felt like a vegetable when it was over—a totally nonfunctioning person," she said. "I was the first person in my family *since the pilgrims* to get a divorce!"

"How did you cope?" I asked.

Thoughtfully, she responded, "The one thing which probably helped me more than anything else was going to church on Sundays. Ever since I was a child, I have gone to church. It was what we did as a family. So, after my divorce, I continued going, regardless of how I felt."

She paused for a moment. "If anyone asked how I was, I told them I was fine, and then I ran to my car and cried alone. I cried all the time. I was really a mess!"

"Don't you think you would have felt better and healed more quickly if you had shared your pain and hurt with others at your church?" I questioned.

"I suppose so, but I was too miserable. Even though I went to church, it took about eighteen months before I could focus on what the minister said. Finally I began listening—to him and to other people, also. I realized I couldn't isolate myself from my church family."

Jeri shifted her position on the sofa, getting more comfortable. "I needed to know I was no less a person than I had been before. As a child I believed God loved me. As an adult that did not change. In fact, I believed He loved me even more because I was hurting, and I needed His love that much more."

"That's a wonderful way to look at it, Jeri," I said.

"God showed me over and over that He is a God of mercy and grace. Once I was past the bad times, I realized God had been close to me all along."

"What about your children?" I asked.

"It is important for my boys to know Jesus like I did as a child. After we coped with Daddy being gone, I worked hard to be a good parent. Two little guys were watching me, and I wanted to help build their faith as mine had been built. They had accepted Jesus at an early age, and I couldn't ignore their need to grow spiritually. So, church became very important to us.

"Strangely enough, one of the benefits of my helping them is that my own faith became more defined. My walk as a Christian has grown much stronger."

A contented silence settled over us as we drank the rest of our coffee.

"You know," Jeri commented, "my divorce has been a good learning experience. It helped me know myself better. The most important part for me and the boys is to know God cares for us and loves us no matter what happens. He'll always be there for us." — L.M.

"For Thou art my hope; O Lord God, Thou art my confidence from my youth."
PSALM 71:5, NASB

Father,
teach us that when tragedies happen in our lives, You reach out to us with your caring love. Thank You. Amen.

✳

Perfect Timing

God doesn't come when you want Him,
but He's right on time.
TENNESSEE WILLIAMS

One of my favorite cartoons shows a person saying, "God, grant me patience and hurry up!" Today, we live in an electronic age of TV, videos, and computers where we can obtain information and entertainment instantaneously. We have instant tea, instant breakfast, and instant microwaveable dinners. We get antsy standing in front of the microwave oven waiting three minutes for our frozen dinners to cook.

Since we don't like to wait for anything or anybody, our timing is often different from God's. However, God doesn't labor under the constraints of our self-determined schedules. He is not bound by time.

An example of this is the biblical story of Noah in Genesis 6—9. Once Noah and his family were in the ark, God closed the door. Most people think that Noah and his family were in the ark for forty days, but the Bible says it rained for forty days. Water flooded the earth for 150 days, and Noah and his family were probably in the ark over a year! God determined when it was time for Noah to come out of the ark.

Like Noah, at times you may feel God has shut the door on you. You may think He is not answering your prayers. If you have been going through a difficult situation for a period of time, you are probably ready to come out of the ark. Perhaps you have done all you thought God was calling you to do, and yet, He remains silent. Times like that truly try our patience. They test our faith.

Although God shuts the door, in His time, He will open it again. Often these doors are not opened as quickly as we would like, but we learn lessons better in the stillness behind closed doors. Sometimes we need to learn more so we can grow by the time God is ready to move us forward.

Another important point in the story is that God gave Noah the specifications for the ark, but Noah was the one who had to build it. God didn't build the ark for him. It was Noah's responsibility to do the work.

God provides us with knowledge and abilities. He expects us to use our learning and talents to glorify Him. God didn't lift the hammer for Noah, and He won't do your work for you. He expects you to do what He has called you to do.

Genesis 8:1 states, "But God remembered Noah. He beckoned Noah to come out of the ark, and He made a covenant with him."

God's rainbow is a covenant with us as well. Every time we see His bow in the sky, we can be reminded that He will answer all our requests—but it will be according to His time. — S.T.O.

"Whenever the rainbow appears in the clouds, I will see it and remember the everlasting covenant between God and all living creatures of every kind on the earth."
GENESIS 9:16

Lord,
teach us to be patient and to learn to wait for Your timing.
Thank You for promising never to leave us. Thank You for
Your rainbow. Amen.

✳

Dormant Bulbs

Men may rise on stepping-stones of their dead selves to higher things.

ALFRED, LORD TENNYSON

My daughter Thelma handed me a box of dormant, ugly, brown bulbs. "Nancy sent these. They're hyacinths which have gorgeous blooms. You can plant them now or wait till spring."

I surveyed the box of dead-looking bulbs with their bound-up roots, finding it hard to believe they would produce beautiful blooms. As I put them away on a shelf, I realized that a few years ago I must have appeared as ugly and lifeless as they did.

When I married, I had dreams of a long, happy life with the man I loved. Bob drank, but I didn't know he was an alcoholic. Why wasn't I warned?

Once we were married, our jobs kept us apart. He worked nights, and I worked during the day. Finally, his schedule switched and he worked days, but he disappeared most evenings. Fortunately, we lived close to the center of town. When he didn't come home after work, I wandered the streets looking in one bar after another, knowing he was spending the money we needed for bills.

When he spent his paycheck, he demanded mine, but I kept it hidden. "How are we going to pay our bills if you drink up all the money?" I asked him.

He stared at me, blurry-eyed, and laughed. "Who cares? Just give me your money!" I couldn't and wouldn't.

Bob was jailed several times for drunk driving. Following one of those lockups, he lost his job. When he received a check for his retirement fund, he cashed it and disappeared. I didn't know where he was for over two weeks. He ended up broke at his parents' house in Arizona, and stayed with them for two years. Finally, he came back, very repentant. He had sworn off drinking. That lasted for three wonderful months, and then it all began again.

When he started speaking crossly to our four-year-old Thelma, she became afraid and didn't want to be near him. I decided I couldn't raise her in that kind of environment. My own stomach churned most of the time because of emotional abuse. A week later, his brother came to visit. Then, Bob returned with him to live in Arkansas.

For two years after our divorce, I felt dead, bound up like the roots on those bulbs. It took that long to get reacquainted with myself and find out who I was.

As time went on, God "planted" me deep in the rich soil of His Word, nurturing and caring for me. My roots unwound and reached down, and I grew in newness of life, flourishing in the love that God showered upon me. His Holy Spirit continues to "grow" me. Hopefully, there have been some blossoms.

When it's planting time, I will enjoy placing those dormant bulbs in rich soil. Blooms will burst forth, bringing fragrance and enjoyment to all who see them. — L.M.

"For behold, the winter is past, The rain is over and gone. The flowers have already appeared in the land."
SONG OF SOLOMON 2:11–12, NASB

Father,
there are times when we feel our roots are all bound up, and
we appear ugly. Help us to hold on until Your spring comes,
and we are loosened to grow and bloom. Thank You. Amen.

✳

The Sudden Urge

Anger is a weed; hate is the tree.
ST. AUGUSTINE

Angrily, I yanked open the car door and slid into the seat. Shifting the car into gear, I screeched out of the parking lot. A burning rage welled up inside me.

I had just attended my youngest son's graduation from high school—alone. This day should have been a joyful family occasion, but my husband and I had separated seven months earlier. We had not seen each other since that awful day in court. My insides were churning. I knew he would attend, but didn't know if he would come alone, or bring the woman he was dating—a woman I had never me.

Just before the ceremony began, my husband entered the football stadium—alone. He walked past where I was sitting, but he didn't see me. I opened my mouth to speak, but the words stuck in my throat.

When the graduation ceremony ended, I jumped up and ran out of the stadium, trying to keep a handle on my emotions until I reached my car. Here I was, behaving like one of the teenagers who normally filled this parking lot, racing my engine and flooring the gas.

When I pulled the car out of the parking lot, a pedestrian stepped out in front of me. In an instant, I realized it was my husband. The first thought that ran through my mind was how easy it would be to hit him—how easy to end my day-to-day trauma of having to deal with him.

In that same instant, I slammed on my brakes. This time, he saw me. A look of horror crossed his face, and beads of sweat broke out on his forehead.

My husband regained his composure, looked the other way, and continued across the street. I realized in that moment that my anger was out of control. When I reached home, I prayed for a better attitude toward him and for my own healing. My anger and rage held me captive and prevented me from getting on with my life.

God didn't heal my anger overnight. In time, as the healing progressed, I finally let go of my anger and bitterness. Today, I have reached a state of acceptance. My ex-husband's actions don't matter to me anymore. Recently, I was seated at a table next to his in a restaurant. He probably wouldn't have spoken to me had I not initiated a conversation. He was moving to another state so I wouldn't see him again for a long time—if ever. I felt no desire to rush out to the parking lot and run away again. With a smile, I said good-bye. — S.T.O.

"Get rid of all bitterness, rage and anger, brawling and slander, along with every form of malice."
EPHESIANS 4:31

Lord,
thank You for helping me close one chapter of my life, so that
another could be opened. Thank You for healing me. Amen.

*

Hang in There, Baby!

The chief purpose [of virtues] is to make us bear with
patience the injustice of our fellows.
MOLIERE

Tears streaked through Darlene's makeup as she talked about her divorce. "My life has been so hard. Have you seen the picture of the kitten hanging onto the knot at the end of the rope? That's how I feel. I married young and thought life would be good. But after a few years my husband disappeared most evenings. He only came home long enough to shower, change clothes, and then leave. It was apparent he was having affairs with other women."

"How did you find out?" I asked.

"Two women who were *friends* admitted it. Their consciences bothered them. There were others, too."

"How did you react?"

"I didn't want him to touch me anymore. Our sex life became abhorrent. That made him angry, so he constantly forced himself on me. Then one day he walked in and said, 'I'm not in love with you anymore.' He left but wouldn't file for divorce. I didn't see him for six months. When I did, he wouldn't give me any explanation."

"Did he send money for food and rent?" I asked.

"No. That meant I had to find work. I enjoyed fixing hair, so that's what I did, but I was only able to make enough to feed the kids and me each day. Until I obtained my license, I did hairstyles for women in churches. I also took other odd jobs. Life was difficult."

"Couldn't you get any help?" I inquired.

"After I filed for divorce, my mother helped when she could. I didn't know where my husband lived, so he was served divorce papers at work. Later, I found out he was living with his latest girlfriend, who was on welfare. He wanted the children so he could make a new family with her. We went through several court battles over custody."

"Who won?"

"He almost did. He told all kinds of lies about me. I had to prove myself a fit mother. Finally, the courts awarded the children to me. He had visiting rights, but he wasn't fair. He moved to Arizona and insisted that I send them at my own expense. He took me to court when he didn't get what he wanted. It was horrible. At the time he had a good job, but he wouldn't send anything for the children. He purposely wanted me to be miserable. If it hadn't been for the Lord sustaining me and giving me the patience to hang on, I would never have made it."

Darlene pulled a tissue out of her purse and wiped away her smeared makeup. At last she looked up and said, "Today, I would have handled things differently, but at least I've learned one good lesson. It took awhile, but now I know that even when my world is falling apart, through God's help, I'll make it. I've 'hung in there, baby,' and that 'knot' is getting easier to hang onto all the time." — L.M.

"Let us run with perseverance the race that is set before us, looking to Jesus."
HEBREWS 12:1–2, RSV

Father,
it's hard to hang on when everything seems to be against us.
Teach us to wait patiently for the accomplishment of Your
working in our lives. Thank You. Amen.

✳

The Soap Opera

Jesus did not say, "You will never have a rough passage, you will never be overstrained, you will never feel uncomfortable," but He did say, "You will never be overcome."
JULIAN OF NORWICH

Do you ever feel your life is like a soap opera? Perhaps you are a single mom with little ones, and "As the World

Turns" you wonder what will happen next? Maybe seven-year-old Karen dropped a gallon of grape juice on your kitchen carpet. Then an hour later, the dishwasher over-flowed, but the soap suds didn't eliminate the telltale signs of the grape stain.

Later, Jimmy and the dog found a skunk in the wood pile, and you discovered another use for tomato juice. Jimmy was easier to clean than the dog.

The next day, you bathed the dog for the tenth time to remove the odor. Suddenly, you realized that it was extremely quiet—a very bad sign. You asked yourself, Where are "All My Children"? After much searching, you found them in your living room, constructing an indoor swimming pool in your sunken fireplace. You tried to decide whether you would like to be transported to "Another World," or if you would just be content with a long stay in "General Hospital."

You finally got "The Young and the Restless" down for a nap, and you sat down to relax and read for an hour. In the magazine advertisements you saw "The Bold and the Beautiful." You glanced in the mirror and you felt neither bold nor beautiful, so you had difficulty identify-ing with that other world where all the children are clean and sparkling and where all the moms look rested and calm and as if they just stepped out of *Vogue* magazine.

Yet, there are "The Days of Our Lives" like when Karen brought you a bouquet of dandelions from the yard and said, "This is my 'Loving' bouquet, Mommie. I love you."

You realize that you only have "One Life to Live," and that even if you *could* change it, you really wouldn't change very much, after all. Your children love and depend on you. You remember the feeling you get when they look up with their trusting eyes and say, "Mommy, I'm happy you are my mommy."

You know that you have a "Guiding Light," and that He will never give you more to endure that you can handle. Life has its trials, and single moms seem to have more than their share. However, problems build perseverance, and perseverance builds character. We become better people through the difficult circumstances in our soap opera lives. — S.T.O.

"You need to persevere so that when you have done the will of God, you will receive what he has promised."
HEBREWS 10:36

God,
we thank You for being our Guiding Light through all the
trials we must endure. Help us to keep our sense of humor
and to become better people as we deal with our
circumstances. Amen.

✳

Fulfilling My Dreams

Blessed are those whose dreams are shaped by their hope . . .
not by their hurts.
ROBERT H. SCHULLER

My dream all through high school was to be a missionary in a Latin American country. I loved excitement and traveling," Debbie said. "My husband and I were both missionary interns. We were so happy when we first married. Then things began to go wrong. Too many outside events got in the way, and our marriage went downhill."

"That's sad," I commented, "especially when you both wanted the same thing."

"I know," Debbie said. "I feared our marriage would end in divorce, and that's what happened. I felt my whole life was over—everything was ruined. My dreams were gone. I didn't think any church would allow me to work for them or go to the mission field after my divorce.

"Then the strangest thing happened. I felt a great need to clean my house and get rid of things. After that, I sensed I should take a leave of absence from my teaching job," Debbie stated.

"I had no idea what I was going to do, but I knew God was going to do something different. After a couple of negative contacts, I learned of a junior high school in Guatemala that needed a mathematics teacher. When I was approved, I only had three weeks to get ready."

"Did you make it?"

"Yes. A couple stayed in my house for the year. My young sons and I packed up and went. My dream came true, except that it was a lonely year. The families didn't know how to handle a single woman with kids. Only one woman wasn't threatened by me. She became a real blessing to our family."

"Did you feel fulfilled?" I asked.

"Yes, but a few years later, I wanted to teach again on a mission trip. I was in the single parent fellowship, and a pastor called me about a short-term trip to Poland. At first I didn't think so, but I went to the information meeting anyway. It sounded interesting, although I didn't have the money. So I boldly told God, 'Okay, if You want me to do this, I have to have a house-sitter, the kids taken care of, and the money to go.'"

"Did that happen?" I questioned.

"Yes," Debbie smiled broadly. "One of my closest friends from college just *happened* to be in southern California during this time and needed a place to stay. My sons were taken care of, and the money came in—all in three weeks!

"My biggest realization was that divorce does not eliminate us from being used by God, and it does not excuse us from allowing Him to make our lives exciting again. Mine has been. When I thought all my dreams were crushed and dead, God gave them back to me in fuller measure than I could have imagined."

Debbie laughed and said, "I'm keeping my bags packed. Who knows where He'll send me next?" — L.M.

"Like cold water to a weary soul is good news from a distant land."
PROVERBS 25:25

Father,
in Your timing, You bless our lives by fulfilling our dreams in
spectacular ways beyond what we believed possible. Thank
You for being a God of surprises. Amen.

✳

Turning Frogs into Princes

For all that has been—thanks. For all that will be—Yes.
DAG HAMMARSKJOLD

Entering the dating game after being out of circulation for a quarter of a century was scary. *How much had men changed in twenty-five years?* I wondered.

I decided never to date a man who wasn't a Christian, but beyond that, I wasn't sure what qualities were important. I made three lists: qualities that were necessary for "Mister Perfect," qualities that would be nice but weren't absolutely necessary, and qualities I promised myself I'd never put up with in another man. As I met single men, I added to my lists. Finally, I reached a point where my "wouldn't put up with" list was twice as long as the other two! I began to have doubts as to whether I would ever find "Mr. Perfect."

One evening when I was feeling particularly depressed, I shared with my wise mentor on his computer E-Mail that I feared I'd have to kiss a lot of frogs to find a prince. I had been on several dates where I found myself wishing I had stayed home and rearranged my sock drawer or some other such exciting activity.

My mentor sent an urgent message back: WARNING: Stop kissing frogs. There are few princes left!

As time went on, I relaxed in my attitude toward dating. At first, I had been looking for "Mr. Perfect" in every man I dated. After a while, I learned to enjoy the company of a variety of men without worrying about whether one of them might become my next husband. Some enjoyed sports, and I'm an avid Angels baseball fan. Some enjoyed theatre, and I have a passion for plays. Plus, I always have enjoyed going out to dinner. What woman doesn't? However, I never deviated from my original premise to only date Christian men.

This brings up another point: Where do you find wholesome Christian men to date? As the number of singles mushrooms in America, many churches are responding with support groups that provide social activities, friends who understand and care, and spiritual sustenance. These Christian singles' groups can be wonderful places to find other singles who have been through similar circumstances and can identify with your problems.

I attended a "Care and Share" group where men and women talked openly about their feelings and concerns. One evening we each painted our own picture of "Mr. or Ms. Perfect." As a result, I realized how important it was not to have standards that no man could ever meet. On the other hand, it was important not to compromise my values in looking for someone compatible.

As the years went by, I discovered how important it was to be content with my singleness before I would be ready for an intimate relationship again. I needed to establish my own identity rather than have my identity solely hinge on a relationship with someone close to me.

I needed to allow others to be themselves. When I dated someone, I tried to accept him for who he was—not for who I wanted him to be. Through this time, I always felt God had someone special planned for me. When I was ready, and my "Mr. Perfect" was ready, God would allow us to meet. — S.T.O.

"All the days ordained for me were written in your book before one of them came to be."
PSALM 139:16

Dear God,
thank You for teaching me to be content with my singleness and for helping me to discover my own identity. Thank You for wisely showing me the important qualities to look for in a mate. Amen.

*

Essential Pruning

Building Sand Castles

The Best Weed Killer

Staying on Track

My Father Understands

Instant Family

I Chose My Baby

Let Go of the Chicken Bone

Ouch!

CHAPTER NINE

Before life becomes fruitful again, there must be a pruning and shaping of our priorities. God wants to be our number one priority. Sometimes He removes our false security so we will depend on Him alone. He brings the tide to wash away the sand castles we build. If we obediently stay close to the Lord through prayer and reading His Word, we keep our priorities in order and stay on track.

*

Building Sand Castles

I don't know much about sand castles. But children do. Watch them and learn. Go ahead and build, but build with a child's heart. When the sun sets and the tides take—applaud.

MAX LUCADO

When my sons were young, they enjoyed going to the beach and building sand castles. We always packed an assortment of different sized plastic glasses and buckets along with some shovels, old serving spoons, and toy soldiers for sentries.

At the beach we searched for sand still moist from the previous night's high tide. Rich and Mike spent hours creating their masterpieces, complete with moats, draw-bridges, and tall lookout points for the plastic sentries.

When they tired of working on their castles, they swam, rode the waves, and searched for shells and inter-esting sea life. Yet, they kept returning to the task of building their creations in the sand. By late afternoon, they had completed their sand castles. The sun became a huge orange ball on the horizon. Its reflection shimmered on the surface of the water. As time passed, the tide rolled in closer and closer to the sand castles. Mike giggled in anticipation. Finally, a breaker crashed into his sand castle and swept it into the sea. Soon a second breaker captured Rich's extravagant creation, leaving only a trace of it in the retreating tide. Rich laughed with delight and asked, "Can we build a fire now and roast wieners and marshmallows?"

The boys weren't surprised that their castles were swept away. They knew it would happen. They picked up their buckets and shovels and turned their thoughts to other things.

Adults are often less wise than children. We build our own sand castles, and when a wave crests nearby, we try to stop it. We lose sight of our priorities. Water soaks our clothing, and salt stings our eyes. Still we shout, "It's my castle. I built it with my own hands. Leave it alone."

The ocean becomes silent, and so does God, it seems. Where did we go wrong? We tried to build our castle in just the right way, but we forgot that God made the sand, and God made the ocean. If we try to build a sand castle by our own strength, He will remind us that our foundation is nothing but shifting sand. If our priorities get out of proportion, He will bring in the evening tide to help reshape the way we see things.

God doesn't mind if we build sand castles, but He doesn't want them to become too important to us—more important than He is. He wants to be the number one priority in our lives.

As Max challenged us, "When the sun sets and the tides take—applaud." We need to place our lives and our sand castles in His hands and trust Him to give us the strength to survive the tides. — S.T.O.

"But everyone who hears these words of mine and does not put them into practice is like a foolish man who built his house on sand. The rain came down, the streams rose, and the winds blew and beat against that house, and it fell with a great crash."
MATTHEW 7:26–27

Lord,
help us to keep our priorities straight. Teach us to depend on Your strength as we shape the sand castles of our lives. Amen.

✳

The Best Weed Killer

Obstacles [weeds] are those frightful things you see when you take your eyes off the goal.

AUTHOR UNKNOWN

Rita waved as she strolled across the park lawn. In her other hand, she carried what I thought was a bouquet of flowers. However, I soon realized it was a bunch of weeds.

"What are you doing with those?" I asked, laughing.

"These are a wonderful object lesson," she answered.

"An object lesson? You must be kidding," I responded.

"No. Actually they have helped me in my Christian life." She laid the weeds on the table.

I waited for her explanation.

"You know the strawberry field out on Bastanchury Road, don't you?"

"Yes," I answered. "I often drive past it."

"The property was leased for years to a Japanese family. They worked hard caring for it. They pulled out weeds, tended the young plants, and supplied water and fertilizer."

"Their strawberries were delicious," I commented.

"One day the woman in the strawberry stand told me, 'This will be our last year to sell berries. Our lease is up, and we're not renewing it.'" Rita paused and then continued, "Soon the strawberry plants were plowed under. The field was left vacant. Before long, I noticed little weeds sprouting up. Day after day, they grew taller and taller until the field was green again. I couldn't believe how quickly all the varieties of weeds took over the whole property."

"I've seen the field. It's a sad sight," I said.

Rita picked up the weeds. "The more I thought about the field, the more I realized it was like my own life."

"What do you mean?" I asked.

"When I tend to my time with the Lord, read His Word, and pray, my life grows beautiful, fruitful plants. When I neglect my devotional time with Him, 'weeds' begin to grow in the once productive soil of my life. Those weeds are hard to dig out, especially if I let them continue to grow. Does that make sense?" she questioned.

"Yes," I answered. "I've had times like that, too. It's easy to stop being watchful—especially of careless words. They seem to take root immediately."

Rita nodded and then added, "I neglect my kids. I slight people when I'm in a hurry. Sometimes I don't show up when I have promised to help someone. Possibly the worst thing is I'm often not loving."

"So where do we get some weed killer?" I asked.

Rita laughed. "I have found God's Word to be the best weed killer I know. Now, with only my kids at home, I can spend the time I need to develop my relationship with God. Beautiful plants are beginning to grow again. I keep some weeds around to remind me!" — LM.

"I will turn toward you and make you fruitful and multiply you."
LEVITICUS 26:9, NASB

Dear Lord,
you know I am prone to let weeds grow in my heart when I
neglect my fellowship with You. Forgive me. Help me root
them out so Your fruitful vines will spring up instead.
Thank You. Amen.

✳

Staying on Track

We make our future by the best use of the present.
MARIE EDGEWORTH

I've camped at some strange places in my life, but one of the most unusual was Pismo Beach, California. Miles and miles of sand dunes line the vast Pacific Ocean as far as the eye can see.

Usually when I camp at the beach, I take my sand chair, a yellow legal pad, and a pen. Upon arrival, I carry these items to the sand, where I spend hours of solitude, sitting on the beach and listening to the waves as they lap at my feet. This setting provides an ideal atmosphere to be creative.

However, Pismo Beach was different. I should have been forewarned when I heard the phrase "camp on the beach" as opposed to "camp at the beach." What a difference a two-letter word can make!

When we set up camp, I pulled out my sand chair and writing materials. Just as I dug my toes in the sand, dune buggies, dirt bikes, and a strange assortment of other motorized vehicles whizzed by me on both sides. I found myself constantly distracted. My mind couldn't focus on the book I was writing with sand flying in my face.

The scene paralleled my life as a single mom. For a long time after my divorce, I had trouble focusing on priorities. Even the most mundane household activities became enormous chores. I had as much difficulty changing gears as did some of the young drivers who threw up sand in a rooster-tail fashion, peppering me and my tablet.

After living in denial for a number of years, I finally learned to face the reality that my marriage was over. No knight in shining armor was going to ride by on his white horse and rescue me just as no beach patrol would rescue me from my present circumstances. I had come to a beach where sunbathers were in the minority and vehicles abounded. I finally faced the fact that I was not in a creative environment, so I put away my legal pad and enjoyed the ocean view and the strange assortment of people riding by.

As I surveyed the vast expanse of water and sand, I became aware of the dominion of God. I determined that my security needed to be anchored in Him—not in money, a vocation, or another person—only in God.

During my recovery, when I finally faced reality and learned to depend on God again, my life returned to order. I developed a plan for doing constructive things that provided quick results. Even little things like planting flowers or repainting my patio furniture brought a great sense of accomplishment.

Although as a single parent, I wasn't exactly where I wanted to be, at this present time, Pismo Beach wasn't exactly where I wanted to be either. However, it was where I currently sat. Again, I pulled out my pen, grabbed my tablet, and went to work. — S.T.O.

"I press on toward the goal to win the prize for which God has called me heavenward in Christ Jesus."
PHILIPPIANS 3:14

Lord,
help me to face the reality of my current situation. Teach me
to develop a plan for my life that includes having You as my
secure anchor. Show me how to be content where I am.

✳

My Father Understands

God has never promised to keep us out of hard places . . .
What He has promised is to go with us through every hard
place, and to bring us through victoriously.
MERV ROSELL

Mrs. Stevens?" a man's voice boomed over the phone at
1:00 A.M. Barb was jarred out of sleep.

"Yes, I'm Mrs. Stevens. Who is this?"

"This is the Highway Patrol. I'm sorry to wake you,
Ma'am, but your husband was in an accident, and he's not
expected to live. You need to come as quickly as possible
to the hospital in Corona."

After she hung up, Barb slumped into a chair and tried
to absorb the shocking news. Then she bundled up her
two sleepy boys and put them in the car. Driving through
heavy fog increased the anxiety weighing on her heart.

When she finally arrived at the hospital, Barb rushed
to the emergency room and inquired about her husband.
A nurse put an arm around her and said, "I'm so sorry,
Mrs. Stevens. Your husband died just a few minutes after
he was brought into the emergency room."

The following days were a blur—preparing for the
funeral and comforting her boys. They didn't understand
what had happened except that their daddy wasn't coming
home anymore.

Barb's marriage to Ron had been difficult, but because
of his untimely death, she felt she was expected to speak
well of him. She felt guilty because she wasn't comfortable
sharing her honest feelings. Consequently, she felt
friendless and alienated at a time when she desperately
needed companionship.

She voiced her frustrations to God. "If only there was someone I could talk to and discuss the problems I had with Ron. It would help me get past them and go on with my life. I feel knotted up inside."

Barb heard about our single parent group and decided to attend. She found people such as herself— some who needed friends to talk with and some who were willing to listen. Gradually the pain began to ease because she was able to share her feelings in a nonthreatening, comfortable atmosphere. Today, Barb is able to reach out and help others because she understands what they are going through.

"One of the best things I've learned," Barb commented later, "is that God is the only One who totally knows and understands me. Through His working in my life, I have found satisfaction because I can depend on Him completely."

We each need to come to that same recognition in our own lives when we meet unforeseen circumstances. If you are having a hard time dealing with your hurts and sorrows, seek the comfort and understanding of your loving Heavenly Father. Ask Him to bring the right people into your life to facilitate your healing. He will. — L.M.

"The Lord is good, a refuge in times of trouble. He cares for those who trust in Him."
NAHUM 1:7

Dear Heavenly Father and Friend,
I know You love me so much that Your ear is always turned toward me. You listen, and You bring others into my life who also listen. Thank You. Amen.

✳

Instant Family

There is no greater invitation to love than in loving first.
AUTHOR UNKNOWN

Hey, Dad, could you throw me a few balls?" ten-year-old Kyle asked his stepfather, Roy.

Roy smiled and grabbed a baseball glove. "Sure, Kyle. Let's do it."

Later that evening, I asked Roy if it was difficult being a stepparent.

He replied, "I had never been married nor had any children of my own when I married Carla. However, for the most part, parenting has been easy. The hard part was making the decision to take the big step."

"Why was that difficult?" I inquired.

"I knew if I married Carla, I wouldn't just get a wife, but an instant family. Kyle was seven at the time, and I struggled with taking on all that responsibility. Plus, I didn't have a seven-year history of dealing with Kyle to draw on. It was scary—not a decision I made quickly."

"I noticed that Kyle calls you 'Dad,'" I said. "I think that's great!"

Roy looked serious. "I didn't let him call me 'Dad' until his mother and I were married. Then I explained to Kyle that I never intended to take the place of his father, and that I never want him to forget who his real dad is. Also, I've been careful not to point out his dad's faults."

"That is really important. How do you and Carla handle discipline?" I asked.

"It is important to set the rules and boundaries while a child is young. I have known Kyle since he was two, and he has always respected me. That helps a lot."

"Does Kyle try to pit you against Carla?" I asked.

"Carla had to learn how to relinquish her solitary authority over Kyle. We now share the responsibility of making him mind. It is vital to set boundaries and stick to them. Carla and I back each other in decisions, and we draw the line where we want it, not where Kyle wants it."

"What happens if you disagree with each other?"

Roy replied, "If Carla thinks I'm being too strict, she tells me in private, not in front of Kyle. We always work out our differences before talking to Kyle."

"You are really involved in Kyle's activities, aren't you?" I asked.

"I try to attend most of his baseball games, and I lead his church youth group. Plus, I set aside time for a quality one-on-one relationship with him."

"What is your greatest joy in stepparenting?"

Roy thought for a moment and then replied, "The greatest joy is being able to show a child unconditional love, asking nothing in return. I couldn't love Kyle more if I had fathered him myself."

I looked at Roy and thought of the love I had seen in Kyle's eyes that afternoon when he called his stepfather "Dad." — S.T.O.

"A wise son brings joy to his father, but a foolish son grief to his mother."
PROVERBS 10:1

Dear God,
teach us to be good parents and stepparents. Help us to uncon-
ditionally love our children, but at the same time to set
boundaries for their behavior. Amen.

✳

I Chose My Baby

*I have often thought morality may perhaps consist solely in
the courage of making a choice.*

LÉON BLUM

You're doing what?" Rochelle shrieked at her husband in
shock. "You're giving me a choice between our marriage
and our baby? I don't believe you!"

"You'd better believe me, because those are your only
choices."

"I want this baby. There is a life growing inside of me,"
Rochelle said as she patted her tummy. "I intend to give
it a chance to live."

Her husband glared at her menacingly. He raised his
arm as though to strike her, but she cowered. "You're not
going to hit me again—ever!" she said. "Especially now
that I'm carrying this baby."

His face contorted in hatred. He narrowed his eyes,
clenched his teeth, and tightened his jaw. "Then that is
that! You made your choice. I'm out of here!" He threw
his clothes in a bag and left.

Rochelle was both scared and relieved. An enormous
weight lifted from her shoulders. She'd endured abuse—
physical, mental, and emotional. However, the thought of
making it on her own financially was frightening.

Three months prior to her husband walking out, when
they had visited his brother, she attended church with her
sister-in-law. She had never gone to church as a child, but
was aware of God. As a young child, she talked with Him
as she played. He was her friend.

That Sunday at her sister-in-law's church, Rochelle
went forward and knelt before God. She told Him she had

done everything she could to make her marriage a success, but had failed. She asked Him to help her work things out.

Three months later the marriage ended. However her closeness to God sustained her during this hard time.

She didn't see her husband again until they met in court for the divorce proceedings. Since he was not interested in the baby, Rochelle signed away her legal rights for child support and alimony. She didn't want him to have any future claims to the child. This forced her to get a job.

After her daughter, Lisa, was born, Rochelle lived with her brother and his supportive family for almost a year. Finally, she was able to move out on her own. One of the first things she did was to consecrate Lisa to the Lord.

One night Rochelle's brother dropped her off at the Boys' Club for some exercise. Someone told her, "Here's the punching bag. Pretend it's your husband. Beat the tar out of him." She did. When her brother came back, she was sitting out in front crying healing tears.

He lovingly placed his arm around her and said, "If I could, I would make the hurt go away. I can't, but remember I'm here when you need me."

It was not a difficult decision for Rochelle to choose her baby over her husband. The consequences of that decision to raise her daughter alone, though, were challenging.

"I don't know how anyone survives without knowing the Lord," Rochelle said. "He is my strength all the time, my friend, and my Lord."

Rochelle made her way through the anguish and survived—so can you! — L.M.

"Those who deal faithfully are His delight."
PROVERBS 12:22, NASB

*Forced choices are difficult, Father—and the consequences
may bring sorrow. When I look to You in confidence, You
guide my way and make everything all right.
Thank you. Amen.*

*

Let Go of the Chicken Bone

Even after God is found, He must be sought.
St. Augustine

As a child, my friend, David, lived in Africa where his
parents were missionaries. He told a story of how he used
to watch African boys catch monkeys. He said, "Catching
monkeys is the easiest thing in the world. Monkeys are
fast. Monkeys are smart, but they have a weakness."

He told how an African boy takes a gourd, dries it,
hollows it out, and then puts a little hole in the gourd just
large enough for a monkey to reach through with his
hand. Then the boy ties a rope to the gourd and to the
base of a tree. Inside the gourd, the boy puts something
the monkey wants, like a chicken bone. Then he walks off
a distance to wait.

Monkeys are curious and aggressive. Soon a monkey
explores the gourd, shakes it, and spies the chicken bone
inside. He reaches his hand into the gourd and grabs the
bone. However, when he tries to remove the bone, he
discovers he can't get it out because the chicken bone has
become wedged in the narrow opening. He pulls and
pulls, but it will not come out.

Then, because the monkey's sole concentration is on
the chicken bone, the little African boy walks up and
catches him. The monkey screams and screams, yanking

on the chicken bone, but he won't let go of his prize. The monkey is caught.

When I heard this story, I thought of my marriage. I held onto that relationship long after I should have let go. I screamed and screamed, but I wasn't willing to let go of my husband. He was my chicken bone. Consequently, I was held captive in an unhealthy relationship which was damaging my health as well as my productivity.

I shouted at God, "Fix my marriage. Change my husband. Restore our perfect little family to what it once was." Yet, I never once asked Him, "Do you want me to stay in this marriage? Is our family life healthy for the boys?"

In time, God had to peel my fingers away from the very thing I wanted most. I couldn't bear the thought of letting him go—of giving him to another woman.

Yet, until I was willing to let go, I couldn't release my hand so God could put something else in it. As long as I spent all my time in mental turmoil over my husband, I couldn't concentrate on what God wanted me to do.

Sometimes God removes our security so we will depend on Him alone. My ex-husband is an executive with a large aerospace firm. As long as I was married to him, I had no money problems, but God knew the time had come for me to sever that tie. He had something better for me.

God asked me to relinquish my control, to let go of my expectations and my pride—to let go of my chicken bone. God does not like to compete with other things in our lives. He wants us to say, "I will not put anything else in place of my desire for You, Lord. I come to You with my hand empty, so You can fill it." — S.T.O.

"Blessed are those who hunger and thirst for
righteousness, for they will be filled."
MATTHEW 5:6

Dear Lord,
help me to let go of those things in my life that are keeping
me from a close relationship with You. Teach me to come to
You with an empty hand, so You can fill it. Amen.

*

Ouch!

Obedience is the fruit of faith; patience the bloom on the fruit.
CHRISTINA ROSSETTI

Most of you have raised a plant at some time," I said to
the Single Parent Fellowship at church one Sunday morning. "It is always a pleasure to watch a plant blossom and
then later to bear fruit or begin a new sprout. However,
there are times when a branch is either broken off acci-
dentally or purposely cut off. What happens to the
branch?"

A voice called out, "It dies."

"Why?" I asked.

Someone else spoke up. "Because it's no longer attached to the plant." Several heads nodded in agreement.

"How long would it take the severed branch to blossom and bear fruit, or to produce a new life?" I asked the
group.

There were frowns on several faces in response to my
question. Then someone said, "It will *never* blossom or
bear fruit."

"Why not?" I asked again.

"Because it can't live by itself," someone ventured.

"Correct," I said. "It is no longer vitally united to the source which supplies its life. Do you all agree?"

"Yes," came a chorus of replies.

I paused a moment and then said, "Jesus said that He is the Vine, and we are the branches. As long as we are vitally united to Him, what happens to us?" I continued questioning.

"We grow and bear fruit," someone said.

"We can become disconnected from Him, whether because of circumstances which we allow to threaten us, or because of our own stubborn will. Sometimes even our friends influence us to separate from Him. What happens?"

"We die," someone affirmed.

"Yes—we die—spiritually," I answered. "We do have control over our reactions to circumstances, which a plant does not. We have the choice of being obedient to God's will or not.

"Is it easy to be obedient consistently so that we are always walking within His will? No, it isn't. Sometimes it hurts immensely, but when we allow anything to separate us from our Vine, Jesus says we are no longer useful. We wither and die. He said that we can do nothing without Him, just as He can do nothing without the Father. Was Jesus ever separated from God, other than on the cross?"

"No," came the answer.

"He knew the importance of obedience so that He was always vitally connected to His Father. God was His life-giving source. He told us plainly that unless we are vitally connected to Him, we have no life in ourselves. We must constantly be on guard over our hearts and lives— particularly when we are single parents. If we continually allow the life-giving current of Jesus' life to flow through us, cleansing and filling us, our lives will richly produce the abundant fruit of His love. — L.M.

"Abide in Me, and I in you. As the branch cannot bear fruit of itself, unless it abides in the vine, so neither can you, unless you abide in Me."

JOHN 15:4, NASB

Father,
we desire to be vitally connected to Jesus always, so that His
life-giving current can flow through us. Teach us obedience
because we know we are helpless without Him. In His name,
Amen.

✳

Setting Boundaries

CHAPTER TEN

We need to learn to say no when others try to compromise our values. Friends become increasingly important, but we must refuse to become involved in unhealthy relationships. When we give God control, we trust His ability to work His will in our lives. He will lead us through the darkness into the light of His love. We can depend on that love.

*

The Face of Hatred

In overcoming an enemy, nothing is more effective than the weapon of love.
AUTHOR UNKNOWN

I hate him. I *hate* him!" I muttered as I drove home from work. My knuckles were white from rigidly holding the steering wheel. This was not dislike. It was hatred, fierce and raw, and it continued to grow. I hated my boss. He was the most insensitive man I had ever known—sarcastic to a fault. He belittled me and constantly put me down, despite how hard I worked at my job. A gnawing churned in the pit of my stomach as working conditions daily became more intolerable. Since I had no one at home to talk to except a young daughter, I was not able to release the hatred and anxiety. It kept building.

My boss was in danger of losing his job because of other inappropriate behavior. His supervisor had already issued several warnings. But if he was forced to leave while my heart harbored my hatred, I knew I would feel miserable and defeated as a Christian. How could I change my attitude toward him? I felt out of control regarding my emotions.

So, I boldly asked the Lord not to allow my boss to leave until He had conquered this hatred in me. Day after day ground by with no relief until one night I picked up a book dealing with relationships. The author wrote that we should *act* toward people we disliked, or even hated, as though we loved them. By doing this, our responses would change, since love is an action, not an emotion.

Hmmmm, I thought to myself. *I wonder if it would work? Something has to be done. Why not try?* So, with determination reinforced by prayer, I began to act. No matter what my boss asked for, I complied cheerfully, giving his work top priority.

In a few days, I found I enjoyed what I was doing. Within a week I was amazed—no more sarcasm. In fact, by the following week, our relationship had developed into a bona fide friendship. Within a month, there was a genuine love between us. God had worked a miracle! When I changed my attitude and actions, my boss changed his.

Two weeks later, he behaved unacceptably when his supervisor came in the office for some information. He was told to have his resignation on the supervisor's desk by 8:00 A.M. the following Monday morning.

How thankful I am that God did not allow me to wallow in my hatred, but prompted me to change while I still had time. That was one of the most advantageous six weeks of my life.

God desires us to obey His commandments to love one another for our own well-being. I learned a much needed lesson. It *can* be done, even in the face of hatred, when we are willing to be obedient. — L.M.

"Hatred stirs up strife, But love covers all transgressions."
PROVERBS 10:12, NASB

Father,
thank You for confronting me with my hatred and placing in
my heart the desire to change that hatred into love. With joy,
in Jesus' name, Amen.

*

The Complacent Frog

The constant challenge in this life we call Christian is the translation of all we believe to be true into our day-to-day lifestyle.
TIM HANSEL

Place a frog in boiling water, and he will jump out. Submerge a frog in warm water, and he feels comfortable. If the water is slowly heated to a higher temperature, he continues in a false contentment because he is not aware of the change. The result is fresh frog legs for dinner.

Kristen told me her life as a single parent parallels the journey of that frog. She said, "If I know something is not right in God's eyes—stealing, for example—I vow not to do it. Like the frog, I jump out of the boiling water. But what about all the lukewarm areas of my life?"

"Why don't you give me an example," I suggested.

"My boss sometimes asks me to tell certain callers things that I know aren't true. I'm tempted to tell his little lies to protect my relationship with my boss. Unfortunately, one lie can lead to another. Soon I am content telling more untruths. The water warms without my even being aware. It's so easy to rationalize my actions."

I looked at my friend with concern. "Apparently this is bothering you, or you wouldn't have mentioned it."

"Oh, Susan, I'm so glad I can talk to you. I wake up in the middle of the night thinking about things I've said to customers—ways I've covered for my boss. I feel like that frog about to be scalded."

"Why don't you confront your boss in a loving way?" I asked. "You should tell him what is bothering you. Set your boundaries, and don't step over the edge."

Kristen looked shocked. "What if he fires me? I've got Kevin's college expenses and Sally's cheerleading costs to consider. I can't let my children down."

"What do you think will happen," I asked her, "if you compromise your values?"

Kristen slumped into a chair and buried her head in her hands. "You are right. How can I be true to God and myself? How can I avoid situations where I am tempted to do what I know is not right? I don't want to be scalded by the boiling water."

I carefully formed my words before speaking. "The first thing you need to do is pray before you approach your boss. Then, inform him that you aren't comfortable making false statements to customers. Hopefully, he will respect your boundaries. Let me know what happens. You need to preserve your integrity."

Kristen confronted her boss and was dismissed from her job. Shortly afterwards, she was offered a similar position with another business.

The last time I saw her she smiled and said, "Because of your advice, I'm sleeping well at night again. I enjoy my new job and know what I am doing is God's will. Thanks for the little nudge to jump out of the pot."

"And when my heart is right,
then you will rejoice in the good that I do."
PSALM 51:19, TLB

Dear Lord,
help me not to fall into a false contentment and allow others
to compromise my values. Teach me to seek Your advice on the
questions that arise in my life. In Jesus' name, Amen.

✳

No Good Men Left!

What is left when honor is lost?
PUBLILIUS SYRUS

I don't care if I never go out with another man in my entire life!" Claire said emphatically as she talked with me.

"Oh, come on, Claire, you don't really mean that—you can't! Men are an important part of our lives." I looked at my friend askance.

"Well, I do mean it. I've had such bad treatment from my ex-husband and the men I've dated since my divorce. I don't think there are any good ones left."

"I think you're wrong," I retorted. "There are many good men in our church singles' group. You should come so you can meet some of them."

"No, thanks," Claire responded.

"What made you so bitter, Claire?" I asked.

"After Bill and I divorced, I was asked out a lot, but most of them only wanted one thing—to take me to bed. When they found out I wasn't interested, neither were they. That was fine with me.

"One really classic incident happened not long ago. This fellow, who was sort of a blind date, came into my front room, looked around, and said, 'Where's your bedroom, and what did you say your name was?' I nearly fell on the floor! He even had the nerve to tell me that if I didn't go to bed with him, I'd never see him again! Can you imagine?"

"That very definitely wasn't the kind of relationship you wanted," I agreed with Claire.

"Aren't there any men who just want to be friends?" she said looking forlorn.

"Yes, there are," I shook my head affirmatively. "You need to come to our singles' group."

Several weeks went by before I was able to convince Claire to come to the Single Parent Fellowship at our church. She ignored the men for awhile. Gradually, as she felt more at home in the group, she began to branch out in the friendships she was beginning to form, even to the point of including some of the men who seemed interested in becoming friends with her.

Claire was deeply hurt during her marriage, and afterwards, by the callousness of the men she encountered. The Lord has worked greatly in her life, bringing His peace and giving her the ability to relate to men in an entirely new way. She became very involved in Bible studies and some of the support groups. She is beginning to share with others, telling them some of her hurts and fears.

We need to concentrate on establishing friendships before we become involved in a deeper relationship. God wants to rebuild a foundation of trust within us so He can bring our lives into conformance with His will. He will help us develop new, healthy friendships.

Recently Claire said, "Thank you for encouraging me to come here. It is one of the best things I have ever done. God has given me a whole new perspective on life."

We shouldn't close ourselves off from people because we fear involvement in unhealthy relationships. On the other hand, we need to be selective when we begin dating again. Our Heavenly Father has the right choices for us if we seek His guidance. — L.M.

"Do not be yoked together with unbelievers."
2 CORINTHIANS 6:14

Lord,
give us wisdom in choosing relationships with others. Teach
us not to fear, but to trust You to lead us in establishing
friendships. Thank You. Amen.

❋

The Attraction

What became of the friends I had
With whom I was always so close
And loved so dearly?
RUTEBEUF

You haven't changed in thirty years!" boomed a voice behind me at the class reunion. I turned around and laughed. There stood the class clown, awarding compliments typical of the ones he issued in high school.

"Hi, Mike! I can't believe it's been thirty years since we graduated." I thought back to a fun time in high school. "Remember when you and two other guys came roaring up my gravel driveway on your motorcycles? My mother almost had heart failure."

"It might surprise her to know that I've turned in my black leather jacket for a white dentist's smock, but on weekends, I still ride my motorcycle."

We both laughed. It was fun chatting with my old friend, but my eyes kept glancing at the front door of the banquet room. I was watching for my high school sweetheart. Of all the people who would be at the class reunion, Chuck was the one who kept slipping into my mind.

As Mike walked away, I glanced at the door once again. Chuck had arrived. I watched him as he walked around the room, shaking hands with old friends. He looked fit and trim with just a hint of a receding hairline in his dark brown hair.

Finally he spotted me and smiled. He walked over and gave me a hug. "Susan, it's good to see you. You look great," he commented.

"I would have recognized you in a minute, Chuck. You look just like you did in high school."

He ran a hand over his receding hairline.

"That's a small price to pay," I commented.

We chatted about our families, common friends, and the toll my divorce had taken on me. As the evening progressed, we talked about our high school dreams and goals. Chuck had become a successful lawyer in a small town in picturesque Maine, while I became a free-lance writer in southern California. We lived two different lifestyles, and yet, we had much in common.

Conversation and personal sharing came easily. It was as though I had seen Chuck yesterday and was bringing him up to date. I remembered why he had been my first love. I wondered how different my life would be today if I had married Chuck twenty-seven years ago instead of the man I had recently divorced.

When my marriage began to deteriorate, I had often thought about Chuck and wondered if he had achieved his dream of becoming a lawyer and if he was happily married. During our conversation, all these questions were answered. Yes, he was happily married with two grown children, and he had a private law practice.

Talking together that evening at our high school re-union, I felt tremendous admiration for the man who had been my first love. Perhaps my singleness added to the intensity of that feeling.

Yet, we both realized that our relationship would go no further than a goodnight hug at the end of the evening. I left my high school reunion feeling like I had reclaimed a long lost friend. — S.T.O.

"A friend loves at all times."
PROVERBS 17:17

Lord,
thank You for the friends You have given to us over our
lifetimes. Thank You for Your guidance in dealing with
feelings and emotions. Amen.

*

An Adventure in the Dark

If you do not know the way, inquire at the Word of God.
JOHN BUNYAN

Oh, No!" Barbara yelled. She held the wobbling car steady as she pulled over to the side of the road. "We have a flat tire, Dillon," she told her young grandson.

"Fortunately, we are not far from your father's house. We'll leave the car here and walk the rest of the way. Then I'll call someone to come and fix it."

Since it was dark, Barbara took her flashlight as they set out on foot. A car raced by—very close, and Dillon held his grandmother's hand tightly. "I'm scared, Grandma."

Barbara squeezed his small hand reassuringly and said, "We don't have to walk far, Dillon. Let's see if we can find a safer place away from the traffic."

Shining her flashlight, Barbara discovered a dirt path several feet off the road. "This will be better," she said. "Don't be afraid, Dillon. Watch the light on the ground from the flashlight. See, it's guiding our feet. That's how God guides us when we read His Word. His light is always right in front of us, showing us one step at a time. Sometimes the way is up and down like this path, or on level ground, but God is always with us no matter where we walk."

"It's hard to see only one step at a time," Dillon said.

"I know," Barbara agreed, "but we have to keep going, because ultimately we will make it. Come on, Dillon, you can do it. Come on!"

Dillon stretched out his short legs to keep up with his grandmother. "I'm trying, Grandma."

"Let's think of this as an adventure. Then it will seem more like fun, don't you agree?"

Dillon looked up at his grandmother and grinned. "Okay, Grandma, but I don't want too many adventures like this one!" They both laughed.

Finally, they came to a hill which was quite steep. Barbara said, "Oh, Dillon, slow down. My body is not in shape, and it's hard for me to climb up this hill. We will have to go slower."

Dillon went a little ways ahead, stopped, and looked back at her. "Come on, Grandma, you can make it. You can do it!" He used her own words to help her along.

What could have been a disaster turned out to be a learning experience for both of them. Later, Barbara thought, *I hope Dillon will always remember our "adventure" when he faces hard situations in his own life.*

Do you have a dark, hilly road to travel? It can be a fearful experience or you can turn it into an adventure, knowing that God is in control and walks alongside of you, using His "flashlight" to light your way. Trust Him.

Call on Him. Let Him lead you through the darkness into the light of His love. — L.M.

> "Your word is a lamp to my feet
> and a light for my path."
> PSALM 119:105

Father,
how thankful we are that we never have to be alone in the
dark. You are always with us. Help us to put on our walking
shoes of faith and step out beside You. In Jesus' name, Amen.

✳

"Why Were You Late?"

So we'll go no more a-roving
So late into the night,
Though the heart be still as loving,
And the moon be still as bright.
LORD BYRON

After a difficult divorce and period of transition, I started dating again. I had been so caught up in making the decision to date that I hadn't given any thought to how my children would react.

My youngest son, Mike, had become my man-around-the-house. He was still living at home after his father moved out. When I accepted my first date, Mike asked lots of questions. "How well do you know this man? Where is he taking you? What time will you be home?"

My oldest son reacted differently. He called from college and offered to coach me. "Mom, I know you haven't dated for a long time. Let me give you some tips on what you should say to these men and what you should watch for. " I was flattered he cared.

The evening of my first big date arrived. Mike resumed his questions. "Did you ask your date where he is taking you? You didn't seem to know when I asked the other night."

"We're going to dinner and to a movie," I answered, thinking that would satisfy him.

However, Mike wasn't finished yet. "What time will you be home?"

"About 11:00 P.M.," I answered defensively. Now I knew how my boys had felt in high school when I quizzed them about their dates.

My first date proved to be a fun evening. The only problem was that the movie lasted three-and-a-half hours. It was 12:45 A.M. when I tiptoed into the house and snuck up the stairs to my bedroom.

Rich was home from college, and both boys greeted me when I walked into the kitchen the next morning. Apparently, they had been having a serious discussion.

Mike frowned and asked, "Why were you late?"

"What?" I replied.

"You said you'd be home at 11:00 P.M. and it was almost 1:00 A.M. when that guy brought you home," Mike stated.

Rich joined the conversation. "Mom, when I was dating and living at home, you made me come up with a better guesstimate than you gave us. You would've screamed if I'd been two hours late!"

"Wait a minute, guys," I said, cutting off my oldest son. "First of all, I'm not in high school. Secondly, I don't keep the kind of tabs on you anymore that you apparently kept on me last night. I trust you and your judgment. If you work late and then take a date out, I don't complain about the hours you keep."

Mike looked concerned, "But Mom, it was your first date."

Suddenly, I realized what an adjustment my dating was to my two sons. I put my arms around both of my boys, "No, Mike, it wasn't my first date—just the first one in twenty-five years. I appreciate your concern, but you guys have to be willing to let me date. Just like I cut the apron strings with you two, you have to trust my judgment. I won't do anything weird, I promise, and I won't embarrass you, either. I promise not to reattach your apron strings if you promise not to hook up mine."

They both smiled.

"It's a deal, Mom," Mike replied.

Rich added, "We love you." — S.T.O.

"Do not let your hearts be troubled.
Trust in God; trust also in me."
JOHN 14:1

Lord,
thank You for children who care. Help me to be empathetic
of their thoughts and emotions in our changing roles of life.
In Jesus' name, Amen.

✳

In the Surgeon's Hands

We cannot really help a person until we have been in the
same furnace of affliction . . . It was said of Jesus, He can
help others because He's been there.
AUTHOR UNKNOWN

You have to have an operation," the doctor said, "as soon as possible. I will set up an appointment for you with the surgeon. My nurse will call you when it's arranged."

I climbed into my car, looked up toward heaven, and said, "Father, we've faced a lot of things together. With Your strength, we will face this together, too."

While I waited for my appointment date, God directed my thoughts to His Son who prayed that His "operation" would not have to take place. "Father, if it is possible—if You are willing—take this cup from Me. I don't want to drink it. If there is any other way. . ." He paused. "Nevertheless, not My will, but Thine be done" (paraphrased from Matt. 26:39).

Three times Jesus prayed. Three times He fell on the ground prostrate before His Father, pleading. Finally, He lifted the cup to His lips and accepted the Father's will.

He wasn't clothed in a gown of white or wrapped in a warm blanket; instead, His stained robe and garments were taken away, and He was left bare. No cap of soft cotton was fitted over His head; someone cruelly crushed a cap of long, sharp thorns upon His brow, causing deep gashes.

A sterile bed with clean sheets was not prepared for His body; only a filthy wooden cross, sharp with splinters, provided a resting place.

There were no surgeons dressed in sterile green gowns to attended Him; rather, dirty Roman soldiers clad in metal and plume-fringed helmets gambled for His clothes. No gloved, antiseptic hands performed the task; rough, unwashed hands administered the tortures He bore.

There were no sterile instruments used at the operating table; instead, huge rough nails were pounded into His flesh. No sedative was given to dull the pain and bring blessed oblivion; a reed of sour vinegar was thrust onto

His lips, gagging Him. No bright light aided the surgeon's eyes; in opposition, the sun gathered clouds around itself and hid its face.

No gentle nurse shook Him into consciousness to check His vital signs; instead, a sharp-edged sword was thrust into His side, verifying His death.

Jesus *died* upon His "operating table."

Even so, He trusted His Father's love to raise Him back to life. He went through the horrors of the valley of death, and yet He still lives. This knowledge was able to give me great confidence on my operating table with not even one moment of fear. The Lord of Peace Himself filled me with calm assurance. How? I don't know. I only know He did.

He held my hand firmly, and He can hold yours just as securely. When we give Him control of our lives, we become confident of His competent ability to work His will in us, regardless of what it is. He is the Lord of life, and we are His workmanship.

We are able to face a serious, even life-threatening, situation knowing that He cares for us personally. We can each place our small, trembling hand in His mighty one and rest in His love. — LM.

"May the Lord of peace Himself continually grant you peace in every circumstance."
2 THESSALONIANS 3:16, NASB

Loving Father,
your peace is beyond our comprehension, but You give it freely
whenever we need it. Help us always to reach out to You with
trust and confidence. Amen.

✳

Loving Too Little, Loving Too Much

They do not love that do not show their love.
WILLIAM SHAKESPEARE

Staring out my hotel window on this winter's day in Washington, D.C., I watched huge chunks of ice lazily drift down the Potomac River. I rubbed my arms and shivered—partly from the cold, but mostly from the memory forming in my mind.

Going through a divorce was the most painful ordeal I have ever experienced. I met my husband at seventeen and fell in love. We were married four years later, and we were happy for about fifteen years. With the addition of two children, our family life flowed smoothly like the Potomac River on a warm, summer day.

Then problems arose—easily solved at first, but more difficult later on. I built an icy wall to insulate myself from the pain. As time passed, I became numb from the cold. I forgot how to love; I forgot how to live. The course of my life became filled with chunks of ice like the Potomac River on this cold, winter's day.

I compared the river with the last time I had seen it during the summer several years before. What a contrast! In the summer, boats charted a course up and down the river, bringing tourists and cargo. Children fished and played on its wide banks. Geese, ducks, and herons dipped into the lazy river to find food.

Today, in the cold stillness below me, I saw no boats, no children, and no fowl. Huge chunks of ice impeded the flow of the mighty Potomac. Like that river, I could no longer be an effective vessel for the Lord if my heart was ice-encrusted—if I was not capable of feeling.

I cried out, "Lord, I never dreamed the death of my marriage would be so painful. I don't ever want to be hurt like this again." I felt as useless as the cold river below me.

I stood at that window, lost in thought, for a long time. As winter passed, the sun would warm the river and bring it back to life again. The boats, the children, and the fowl would return.

I needed to let go of the icy wall in my heart, too. I needed to allow God to warm me, to work in my heart and my life again. To help others, I needed to be able to empathize with them. To love others, I had to become vulnerable once more. I knew I could not accomplish these goals in my own strength.

Loving too much leaves us open to the danger of being hurt, but loving too little can cause us to forget how to love and forget how to live. — S.T.O.

"Let us not love with words or tongue
but with actions and in truth."
I JOHN 3:18

Dear Lord,
I don't want to possess an icy heart. Allow Your love to warm my heart that I may be an effective vessel, bringing Your love and hope to others. Amen.

✳

Growing in Strength

A Beacon of Light

Patience Perfected

Flying in Formation

Centered in Turmoil

Flying Solo

Redeeming the Hurt

Angels: Seen and Unseen

Build the Stack Strong

CHAPTER ELEVEN

God is our comforter and our strength, but He realizes that we need other people to love us and encourage us. Peace and trust become ours as He brings significance and stability back into our daily living. As we heal and grow in His strength, we can shine like a beacon from a lighthouse, providing an example for others. Often God uses the very thing that scarred us to heal the wounds of others. Our safety lies in God's protective arms.

*

A Beacon of Light

You are writing each day a letter to men;
Take care that the writing is true.
It's the only gospel some people may read,
That gospel according to you.
WALLACE E. NORWOOD

Shivering, I zipped my blue windbreaker tightly around my neck. The damp air chilled me as I stood watching the fog roll in. I began to walk faster along the shore, hoping that an increased heart rate would mean greater warmth to my body. Darkness was quickly settling in, but I felt determined to take my nightly walk. This was my quiet time.

The clouds overhead blocked the moon, so I carefully picked my way across the rocky portion of the beach to the sandy stretch. In the distance, I saw the beacon from the lighthouse on the point. I used its flashing light to guide me.

How often my life revolved like that beacon, so busy and yet going nowhere. As a single parent with two sons, I had to work outside of my home. I often felt stress from the many demands on my time.

I continued walking toward the lighthouse. As I stared at the circling light, it began to take on a new significance to me. Because of one bright light, captains would know how far from shore to sail to avoid crashing on the rocky reefs that jut out from the point. That lamp warned all the passing ships and guided them to safety.

Watching that revolving beacon, I felt a close identity with it. Many of the people who pass through my life are not Christians. Like the ships, they might steer close to dangerous rocky places. Sometimes they seek advice. Could I set priorities that would influence their lives by the Christian example of my own life?

The steadiness of my inner peace and strength come from the Lord. If I share this with them, they may desire to know Him better. At that moment, I determined my goal would be to radiate light like the powerful beacon.

What about the example I am setting for my children? Am I so preoccupied with my work that I tune them out when they talk to me? Instead of ignoring them, I should use those precious moments to listen. Our conversations could be channeled to draw our family closer together and nearer to God. I vowed to concentrate on listening more carefully to my children in the future.

Finally, I reached the lighthouse. It was time to turn around and start back. However, I lingered for a moment, gazing up at the powerful light. Grasping its awesome responsibility, I thought of my own. Tomorrow I would try to imitate that beacon, shining brightly to help those who cross my path. — S.T.O.

"Shine out among them like beacon lights, holding out to them the Word of Life."
PHILIPPIANS 2:15–16, TLB

Dear Lord,
help me to reach out to those around me with Your love.
Please allow me to be a beacon, reflecting Your light. Amen.

✳

Patience Perfected

The strongest of all warriors are these two—
Time and Patience.
LEO TOLSTOI

Marie, I think you have a problem. You seem to run from one man to another." My friend, Marie, had dated at least a dozen different men in the last two months.

"I need to find someone who cares for me. I'm out there looking all the time," Marie responded.

"Why?" I questioned her.

"Everyone is getting married but me. I'm lonely. Last month I went to four weddings in our singles group, and this month there are two more. Why not me? What's wrong with me?" Marie implored.

"There's nothing wrong with you. You need to cultivate some patience, that's all," I responded.

"I've tried, but I become so anxious. Maybe God isn't hearing my prayers," Marie said, looking dejected.

Watching her, I sensed her agony. Finally I put a hand on her shoulder. "You know, Marie, just about everything in life that is important takes time. How many people have instant gratification? Think about it. You wait to start school. Then you wait for high school and college. It takes time to find a job. You turn in a resume and wait for an interview. If you get married, you have to wait. . . ."

Marie interrupted me. "Yes, I know all that, but it doesn't satisfy my need for someone right now."

"Your *need* is to slow down," I remarked. "In the Bible it says God will give us perfect peace when we set our minds to think about Him. Have you tried that? We learned that verse last year, remember?"

Marie hung her head. When she looked up at me, tears glistened in her eyes. "Oh, Lucille, you're right. I forgot. God also *gives* us patience, doesn't He? I think that's somewhere in the Bible, too. I've tried to find someone by myself, thinking God isn't interested in me. I've really been stupid, haven't I?"

"No, my friend," I replied, putting my arm around her. "You're focusing on the wrong object, that's all. You're looking at men and not God. God is interested in our relationships because He cares for us. If it is His will for us to marry, He has the perfect mate picked out. Our part is to wait and prepare ourselves so we'll be ready when God provides. Are you ready for a serious relationship?" I asked, looking at Marie.

For a moment Marie stared back at me. Then she smiled and shook her head. "I've never thought about it that way. I'm not ready for 'Mr. Wonderful.' I'm glad you were here to talk some sense into me." Marie jumped up from the kitchen table, picked up her purse, and called back over her shoulder as she left, "I'd better go to the bookstore so I can begin reading about having patience."

I watched her race down the sidewalk. "Yes, my friend," I said laughing. "You'd better hurry so you can learn how to wait." — L.M.

"Rest in the Lord and wait patiently for Him."
PSALM 37:7, NASB

Father,
remind us when we sit back and allow You to direct our lives,
You have the answers to our questions and needs. Teach us to
rejoice and praise You. Thank You. Amen.

✳

Flying in Formation

Birds of a feather will gather together.
ROBERT BURTON

In the spring, geese instinctively form a V-shaped formation when they fly north. As each bird flaps its wings, it reduces the wind resistance on the bird behind it. Thus, each goose cuts an easier path for the one following it. This allows the flock to cover a greater distance than if each bird flew on its own.

Those of us who are single parents can be compared to this flock of geese. As single moms, we are traveling in a common direction. Most have been through a turbulent divorce and are on the road to recovery and wholeness. Many have the added responsibility of raising their children alone.

If we travel on the thrust of one another like the geese, then we are moving together toward recovery. If we uphold each other, then our path is smoother. We don't feel the air turbulence or the down drafts so severely if someone is directly in front of us.

If a goose gets out of formation and tries to journey alone, it quickly feels the force of the wind on its face, and its pace is slowed down. It naturally senses its error and moves back into formation to take advantage of the shelter of the bird immediately in front of it.

Often we do not show as much common sense as our feathered friends. We try to "fly alone" saying, "I'm fine. I can handle all my problems myself. I don't need anyone else."

God does not mean for us to "go it alone." He is our comforter and our strength, but He realizes that we need other people to love us and to encourage us. We see Him best through others. His light shines through their caring, their listening, and their understanding.

It is hard for those of us who have always been leaders, who have always directed the gaggle, to learn to depend on someone else. We are used to guiding others, not in seeking help ourselves. Sometimes God must humble us to get us to the point where He can use us.

When the lead goose becomes weary, it drops back in the formation and allows another goose to fly point. Yet, we continue to beat ourselves to death, refusing to give up the lead. We can learn a valuable lesson from our graceful friends in the sky if we, too, learn to fly in formation.

The geese at the back of the formation honk to encourage those in front of them to keep going. Let us "honk" to comfort each other and to encourage each other. — S.T.O.

"Carry each other's burdens,
and in this way you will fulfill the law of Christ."
GALATIANS 6:2

Lord,
teach us to love and encourage one another. Help us to learn
to fly in formation, thankful and dependent on those You
have sent to share our journey. In Jesus' name, Amen.

✳

Centered in Turmoil

There are times of . . . central peace, subsisting at the heart
of endless agitation.
WILLIAM WORDSWORTH

Famous artists from many countries entered a contest to capture the meaning of "peace." The winner was to receive a valuable prize.

Some of the drawings portrayed the following:

➤ Horses grazing contentedly in a meadow as fleecy clouds floated by

➤ A cat snoozing on a sunlit window sill

➤ A frolicking stream bubbling its way down a hillside

➤ A multicolored butterfly gracefully spreading its wings over a flower

➤ A magnificent sunset spilling its colors over the earth

➤ A grandfather and grandson sitting on the bank of a lake, dangling their fishing poles in the water

➤ A mother smiling at the sleeping child in her arms

➤ A crystal-clear lake nestled at the base of a majestic mountain

Many more pictures portrayed quiet, restful scenes. The judges examined the pictures carefully and finally made their choice. None of these gentle scenes won.

The prize-winning painting depicted a turbulent, tumbling waterfall, cascading wildly over a steep bank. Wind whipped the water in a swirling frenzy. Behind the waterfall, a small tree jutted from the steep cliff. Balanced precariously on one of its branches, a nest had been built where a mother bird sat tending her little ones.

At any moment, the wind and water could have whisked the nest away, plunging it to the depths of the waterfall and smashing it against the rocks. It was a place of great danger, and yet the mother bird sat serenely on her nest, seemingly oblivious to the danger.

That picture won unanimously.

Do you and I have that kind of peace as single parents—being serenely at peace, tending our families while utter chaos surrounds us?

The dictionary defines peace as a state of tranquility or quiet, freedom from disturbing or oppressing thoughts or emotions. Well-known pastor, Charles Stanley, stated that peace is contentment in time of trial. My favorite definition of peace is solid quietness.

Is the rent due, and you don't have enough money? Has your car broken down? Did you lose your job? Is one of your children ill? Do you find handling your own finances stressful? No matter what is happening, you *can* be in a state of tranquility.

Jesus alone is able to grant us this kind of peace, since He is the "Lord of Peace." He protects and supports us in every circumstance, including the worst of trials. Our part is to allow Him to undergird us with His peace.

His peace is available to each of us. He waits to give it to us. Reach out for your portion today. — L.M.

"Be like a dove that nests beyond the mouth of the chasm."
JEREMIAH 48:28, NASB

Father God,
how greatly we need Your peace to stabilize us daily. Enable us to cope with each problem that arises and meet it triumphantly through Jesus, our Lord of Peace. Amen.

✳

Flying Solo

Challenges make you discover things about yourself that you never really knew.

CICELY TYSON

While the Boeing 737 banked on takeoff, I stared out the window at the twinkling city lights below. I enjoyed watching the lights disappear, hidden by the clouds as we gained altitude.

The airplane leveled off and headed for Southern California. Laying my head back in the seat, I recalled some family memories of my boys growing up—beach picnics, camping on the Colorado River, swim meets.

For many years, we had a "model family life," filled with love and emotional support for one another. Then something went drastically wrong. Slowly, I felt an enormous gulf stretching between myself and my husband. Eventually that chasm became too wide to cross. To do so would have meant compromising my faith and my entire value system. The price was too high and was not one I felt the Lord wanted me to pay. Divorce seemed the only alternative.

Working day and night, I threw myself into my profession. I welcomed chances to get away to teach at writers' conferences around the nation. By physically leaving my home, I tried to leave all my problems behind.

Although that didn't happen, eventually I did work through the devastation of divorce. The emotional support of my boys and my loving Christian friends brought my world back into perspective.

One important fact I realized was that the boys and I were still a family. A family doesn't have to have an earthly father present to be whole, since our Heavenly Father is always with us. Not having my husband to rely on anymore helped me learn to depend on my Lord.

When everything was going well in my life, I thought I was somehow responsible. It was easy to develop a feeling of overconfidence and complacency. However, when the walls came tumbling down, I was forced to depend completely on God.

As the airplane soared through the sky, I realized how drastically my perception of home had changed. Home used to mean cooking dinner for my family and waiting for everyone to gather around the table in the evening for a time of sharing. Now my sons were grown, and I was returning to an empty house. Even so, I enjoyed the thought of coming back to the familiarity and quiet of my home.

When I walked through the front door, I would be alone. Yet, how much more lonely an empty relationship is than being alone physically. God has healed me and filled me with His presence. I no longer feel lonely when I am by myself, and coming home is wonderful. — S.T.O.

"Those who hope in the Lord will renew their strength. They will soar on wings like eagles; they will run and not grow weary, they will walk and not be faint."

ISAIAH 40:31

Dear God,
thank You for teaching me to depend on Your strength, instead of on my own. Thank You for teaching me the difference between being lonely and being alone. Amen.

✳

Redeeming the Hurt

*Spiritual milestones are victories and accomplishments the
Lord has given us as we journey through life.*
STUART P. BOEHMIG

Talking with Midge, I soon sensed her hurt. "How long
were you married, Midge?" I asked.

"Twenty-six years. We had three daughters and a son.
I never felt secure. I had been abandoned as a child, so I
wanted my marriage to be perfect." She sighed. "But after
twenty years, our problems escalated. I kept trying even
though things were bad. It's interesting, though, that
those problems—in time—brought me to the Lord."

"How so?" I asked.

"When I finally realized how strained our lives were,
I sought counseling. My husband went a few times but
wouldn't participate. He sat with his arms folded and his
ears closed. Mentally, he just wasn't there.

"My older brother had waited for ten years to talk to
me about the Lord. The time never seemed right until my
marriage was floundering. When he witnessed to me, I
decided to turn my life over to God. I figured if I did, God
would make everything all right. Later I realized I had
been living in a fantasy world, and I needed to grow up.

"My husband wanted to stay in the marriage, but he
was not there for me emotionally. Counseling helped me
understand this. My eyes began to open, and I had to look
at my life. As bad as things were, I knew God was there
no matter what happened to us.

"I started going to church and Bible study, but my
husband wouldn't attend. When he finally decided on a
separation, he packed his bags and left."

"That must have devastated you," I commented.

Midge nodded her head. "He quickly found someone else. After a year he filed for divorce. Because of the children, we still saw each other, but any relationship between us was over. I had no choice in the matter."

"How did your children feel?" I asked.

"Abandoned. They were in denial like I was."

Midge continued, "I knew I must support myself and my kids, so I returned to college for a degree."

"What did you major in?"

Midge smiled. "Would you believe I have a Masters in Marriage and Family Counseling, and I am a licensed counselor? I also authored a book on the same subject."

We both laughed. "You took your divorce seriously and used it to benefit others."

"God showed me I could go forward and live a normal life. He faithfully helped me develop into a person I could be proud of. It's been an exciting journey. I can see God's touch in my life and in the lives of those I counsel."

Regardless of what has happened, God can use the very things that wounded you to heal the scars of others. When you trust Him with your hurts, He can build significance back into your life. — L.M.

"He changes a wilderness into a pool of water, And a dry land into springs of water."
PSALM 107:35, NASB

Father,
You have counseled me and brought significance into my life.
Thank You for training me to do the same for others.
In Jesus' name, Amen.

✳

Angels: Seen and Unseen

*I have held many things in my hands, and I have lost them
all; but whatever I have placed in God's hands, that I still
possess.*

AUTHOR UNKNOWN

A still, small voice inside told me to pray for Mike, my
youngest son, as I lay in bed late one Saturday night. I was
five hundred miles from home, teaching for a week at a
writers' conference. Yet, I felt an urgency to pray for him.

Mike celebrated his twenty-first birthday that evening. Three years before, he had responsibly assumed the
role as my man-around-the-house after his father moved
out. So when he asked if he could have a few friends over
to celebrate his birthday, I said, "Sure."

When I returned home, Mike told me that several
unknown high school students crashed his party. My son
and his six-foot-plus friends ushered them out the door.

Later, accompanied by forty local gang members, they
returned with guns, knives, sledge hammers, and crow-
bars. Mike and his friends stood in the living room, staring
out the window in disbelief as the sound of breaking glass
filled the air. The gang threw bricks and potted plants
through the front glass panes. Reacting quickly, Mike
raced upstairs and dialed the police emergency number.

A brick crashed through the front window and sailed
across my ceramic angel collection in the living room. It
hit the wall with such force that it left a hole before falling
to the carpet. A second brick followed. Then a third.
However, not a single, fragile angel was damaged.

Although these violent young people broke the dead
bolt and shattered all four glass panes in the front door,

something kept them from entering the house and harming my son and his friends.

Other members of the gang broke the windshields and beat on the cars parked in the driveway. When the police arrived ten minutes later, the gang members scattered, leaving over ten thousand dollars in damages behind.

The flower pots, front door, and windows could be replaced. Even the badly damaged cars in the driveway could be repaired, but lives are not so easily mended. Fortunately, not one of Mike's friends was harmed.

When I fell asleep that night, unaware of what was happening at home, I felt God's peace. Now I know why. His host of angels protected my son and his friends, many of whom I had known since they were five years old. Nary an angel, ceramic or "real," was harmed.

We don't always know what will happen each day. Sometimes we are far away from our loved ones and the crises they endure. However, God has assured us that He is always with them and with us. His angels stand watch day and night. We can rest in this assurance. — S.T.O.

"For He will command His angels concerning you to guard you in all your ways; they will lift you up in their hands, so that you will not strike your foot against a stone."
PSALM 91:11–12

Dear God,
help us to remember that You are our fortress and security.
Our safety lies, not behind closed doors, but only in Your protective arms. Amen.

✳ ❧

Build the Stack Strong

Give us grace and strength to forbear and to persevere.
ROBERT LOUIS STEVENSON

Be careful how you stack that wood, Al," Herb told his son. "Place each piece securely on top of the one below, or the whole stack is going to fall over. It has to be perfectly balanced to be strong."

Marsha, sitting nearby reading, had come to Uncle Herb's home in the mountains for a short vacation. She paused in her reading, mulling his words over in her mind.

Hmmm, she thought, *maybe that's what happened to our marriage. We didn't put the pieces together securely, so it toppled over. It wasn't perfectly balanced.*

Marsha was married for fifteen years, but in time, she and her husband drifted apart. There was no feeling left, so they divorced.

Marsha did considerable reading on reasons why marriages fail. She began to realize several things which had caused the breakdown of her own.

That evening, Marsha wrote out a list of tools for a solid marriage. She gave this careful thought, since she was dating a man who might be serious about her. She set down a list of basics she felt was essential:

1. Spend time communicating who we are and what we want out of our marriage, being completely honest with each other;

2. Read and study God's Word together daily.

3. Be faithful in our church attendance;

4. Pray together, being specific about our needs and those of our loved ones and friends;

5. Talk it out when we are upset with each other, and always be forgiving;

6. Be aware of our differences as man and woman and accept them;

7. Be affectionate—say "I love you" often.

8. Continually build each other up with our words and actions.

Marsha put her pencil down for a few minutes and looked back over the list. *I think I've left out the most important aspect of all,* she said to herself.

9. *Constantly express our love for God and for Jesus.*

Marsha revised her list, rearranging her priorities. She shared it with her aunt and uncle the next morning at breakfast and received hearty approval from both of them.

"You know," Uncle Herb said, "too many young couples forget the common basics of decency when they get married. They think everything will fall into the right places, but it doesn't without work and determination."

"Yes," Marsha added, "it's just like your stack of wood, Uncle Herb. All the building blocks of a marriage must be placed securely on top of each other. Then it will be strong, stable, and enduring despite any storms that come. Thank you for showing me that." — L.M.

"Then they said, 'Let us arise and build.' So they put their hands to the good work."
NEHEMIAH 2:18, NASB

Father,
too often we build without using the proper ingredients to
make the walls of our marriage secure and strong. Master
Builder, we need Your blueprints and direction. Amen.

✳

Celebration of Love

Unselfish Love

The Gift

I'm Ready to Love Again

I Call Him "Dad"

Lavish Love

Happily Ever After with Detours

His Heart of Love

A Thousand Ways

CHAPTER TWELVE

Living happily ever after includes our reaching out to others in love. This sometimes entails sacrifice, but this, too, brings wholeness as we rely on God's love and give lavishly out of our love for Him. Our Heavenly Father's love and understanding extend to each of us in the same way. We are going to make it! What we thought might be an ending truly becomes a new beginning.

*

Unselfish Love

You can give without loving,
but you cannot love without giving.
AMY CARMICHAEL

Please don't cry anymore, Mother. Your God will work
things out. He will provide, as you have said many times."
Ruth lovingly placed her arms around her mother-in-law's
shoulders and held her.

"Oh, Ruth, God has dealt us a bitter blow. First my
husband died. Now both of my sons are dead. What have
I done to deserve this? We left our home because of the
famine. Living in this country ten years has taken a great
toll on us." Ruth, now also a widow and childless, clung
to her mother-in-law. As the days passed, Naomi talked
more and more of returning to the land of Judah. News
came that God had again provided food for His people.
Naomi decided to return home.

Ruth could not bear to watch Naomi leave. She was at
a crossroads in her life and must make a decision. Should
she stay safely in Moab with her family or step out in faith
and follow Naomi to a strange and foreign land? Would
Naomi's God truly provide, as she had bravely told her?
Ruth weighed her options and made her choice.

"I will go with you, Mother," she said gently.

They made preparations and began their journey.
However, Naomi stopped along the way. "No, my daughter," she said, "do not leave your family. Go back. God will
be kind to you as you have been to me. He will help you
find another husband."

Ruth looked longingly at Naomi and said, "Don't ask
me to return. Allow me to go with you. I want to live with

you and be part of your family. I desire your God to become my God. You are closer than my own mother, and I love you."

Naomi gave up urging her to stay, so they traveled to Bethlehem and lived in Naomi's former home.

At times Ruth wondered if she had made the right decision. It was a difficult life, but she began to see God's hand providing for their needs. Then Naomi skillfully arranged a new marriage for Ruth—a marriage to a relative named Boaz who could redeem Naomi's property so it would remain in the family. He became their "kinsman-redeemer."

Ruth made the choice to unselfishly give up her own family to follow Naomi and her God. If she hadn't, we might never have heard of her.

Ruth's devotion and loyalty to Naomi were instrumental in her becoming the great-grandmother of King David, who carried in his lineage *our* great kinsman-redeemer, the Lord Jesus Christ. Because of His love for us, He redeems our lives by forgiving our sins and promising us life eternal with Him.

Often when we become single parents, we are called on to make difficult decisions between following the easier way or stepping out in faith, trusting that God will provide for us and our children. He can surprise us in greater ways than we could ever imagine or plan for ourselves. — L.M.

"Do not urge me to leave you or turn back from following you; for where you go, I will go, and where you lodge, I will lodge. Your people shall be my people, and your God, my God."
RUTH 1:16, NASB

Father,
if love should call me to follow Your leading, help me to give
unselfishly so that Your purposes can be fulfilled in my life. In
Jesus' name, Amen.

✳

The Gift

You give but little when you give of your possessions. It is
when you give of yourself that you truly give.
KAHLIL GIBRAN

Awakening to the bright California sun streaming in my window, I realized it was my first Christmas morning as a single parent. I had been separated for less than two months and dreaded the approaching holiday season and all the emotions aroused by past remembrances.

In spite of our tight finances, God had provided some extra money so I could buy my young men some needed items as well as some fun ones. My oldest son, Rich, was home from college for a week. My youngest son, Mike, was on his high school Christmas break. We were enjoying some quality time together before our busy schedules resumed.

Later that morning, after a breakfast of our favorite homemade coffeecake, we sat around the Christmas tree, opening our presents.

"You know, Mom, even though there's less under the tree this year, somehow it seems to mean more," Rich said. "Being home for the week with you and Mike matters a lot, too. Funny, I just took all this for granted before."

"I'll be honest, guys. I've been a little apprehensive about the holidays. There have been so many changes in our lives the past two months, and I know the divorce has been almost as hard for both of you as it has for me." I paused, trying to put my emotions into coherent thoughts.

Mike decided to share his feelings, too. "I was afraid somehow that we wouldn't be a family anymore. I mean, that we wouldn't feel like a family or something, but that hasn't happened."

"We *are* still a family," Rich added emphatically.

"Just being together is what matters," I added. "I really enjoyed having both of you here for the midnight service at church last night." With Rich 150 miles away, we didn't get a chance to worship together very often anymore.

After most of the packages were opened, Mike handed me an envelope for my last present. It was his Christmas gift to me. I knew he hadn't been working many hours, so his finances were even tighter than mine. Water polo season had just ended, and I wanted him to keep up his studies, so he only worked a handful of hours each week lifeguarding at our local pool.

I looked up and Mike's eyes met mine. "Well, open it," he said.

I did. Inside the envelope was a handwritten gift certificate that read: Good for one oil change and a tire rotation.

Tears filled my eyes as I hugged my youngest son. Mike's gift would save me money, which would help my tight budget. However, it meant far more than that. Mike had given me the greatest gift he had to offer—his time, himself.

As I pondered the sacrifice my son was willing to make for me, I felt totally at peace on this special Christmas Day.

I was reminded that God also made a sacrifice that first Christmas when He gave us the greatest gift He had to offer—His Son. — S.T.O.

"For God so loved the world that He gave His one and only Son, that whoever believes in Him shall not perish but have eternal life."
JOHN 3:16

Lord,
thank You, for the precious gift of Your Son, and thank You
for my wonderful sons, also. Guide us as we learn the joy in
giving of ourselves. Amen.

✳

I'm Ready to Love Again

There exists in the heart of every person who loves life
the thrill of a new challenge,
the insatiable appetite for what is coming next.
GARY P. BISHOP

At a writers' conference a few years ago, I met a gentle, caring man who had come to find a publisher for his book. He had written about his daughter who had died needlessly. An instant friendship developed between us, and we enjoyed spending time together at meals and programs and talking about our aspirations as writers.

Even though our friendship never developed further, I realized after the conference was over that I was ready to love again. It had been a number of years since my divorce. Although I was never involved in therapy, I knew God had slowly healed me over the years.

Being involved in the Single Parent Fellowship at church had also added to my well-being. The friendships formed there have been vitally important to me. Some of them will last forever.

Where is the Lord taking me from here? I don't know. But I enjoy my life and am delighted with what He is doing in me.

It would be nice, however, to have someone to open my heart to and to share my life with, growing together in studying God's Word and praying. It would be a pleasure to help each other when hurts or trials rear their heads. It would be a blessing to lift each other to reach higher potentials than we would have if we were alone.

My heart is ready to reach out for a special love. However, if that never happens, I will still be satisfied and fulfilled, content to remain as I am. I know that the real lover of my total being is always present, supplying an abundant amount of His love in my life.

Even if God does not have anyone in store for me, there is still Someone always with me, to read the Word and pray with, Someone to be with me in every aspect of my life. He is there, eager to share my every thought and desire. He made me, so He knows me inside and out, far better than I know myself, and He is aware of my weaknesses and my strengths. In His wisdom, He knows what is best for me as I strive to follow Him in loving obedience.

It is comforting to know that even if God so ordains that we live alone, He is always there, reaching out in His love and compassion, and He will supply our *real* needs. We may not have all the advantages our married friends have, but Paul said that when we are single, we can devote our time to the Lord. That can be an exciting prospect, because every day is a new day with fresh opportunities and possibilities.

I'm ready for whatever God has prepared for me. How about you? — L.M.

"In Him you have been made complete."
COLOSSIANS 2:10, NASB

Father,
I don't know the direction You are taking my life, but You do.
I am satisfied with whatever Your plans are, because I know
they flow out of Your great love for me. Thank You. Amen.

✳

I Call Him "Dad"

Example is not the main thing in influencing others.
It is the only thing.
ALBERT SCHWEITZER

Alex sat in a classroom, confused about what was happening to him. His mother had recently moved him across the country from California to the east coast. The six-year-old looked at his new teacher and pleaded, "Where is my daddy? When can I see my daddy again?"

The teacher's reply was cold, and uncomforting. "You won't be seeing your father. Your parents got a divorce." Alex had never heard the word "divorce" before, but that word would echo in his mind for the next fifteen years.

Within the year, Alex's mom remarried, and Alex had the added problem of adjusting to a new stepfather. Bob was totally different from his real father. He also had a beard, which Alex found intimidating at first. Slowly, the kind, gentle man won the confidence of his new stepson.

Their family life went smoothly for a while until Alex found out his mother was expecting a baby. When telling his story to me, Alex said, "I was afraid my mom and Bob would love my stepbrother more than me. However, I soon realized that wasn't the case.

"Mom was afraid I would be jealous of him, but I wasn't. She allowed me to help care for the plump, little guy. I held his bottle and helped bathe him. I ran errands for Mom, picking up the things she needed to feed, dress, and change my little brother.

I got so caught up in the process that I didn't have time to be jealous. Plus, Mom always read to me while she fed him and talked to me while she performed the other chores. When a second stepbrother came along, we did the same thing, and I never gave my original fears a second thought."

"That's great," I responded, "But how did your step-father react to having two sons of his own?"

"I was afraid that Bob would give me less time or show favoritism to his own sons, but that never happened. When he bought a present for my stepbrothers, he bought one for me, too. If they got seven presents for Christmas, I got seven presents. Bob was careful to treat us equally."

"What is the most important thing you remember about growing up with Bob?" I asked.

Alex thought for a moment before replying. "The one-on-one time Bob spent with me affected me the most. Each week, he would set time aside for the two of us. We'd play catch, go to lunch, or buy ice cream cones. He continued spending weekly time alone with me until I graduated from high school."

"Have you seen your birth father since the divorce?" I asked.

"Yes, there have been a few occasions when our paths have crossed. However, the time together seemed awkward. I never really got to know him as a father. My stepfather has done all the things a father should do for his son. That's why I'm proud to call Bob 'Dad.'" — S.T.O.

"Love does not delight in evil but rejoices with the truth. It always protects, always trusts, always hopes, always perseveres."
1 CORINTHIANS 13:6–7

Lord,
Help us to love and accept our children—whether from birth or a blended family. Teach us to form parallel relationships as our children grow taller and wiser. Amen.

*

Lavish Love

Give all thou canst; high Heaven rejects the lore of nicely calculated less or more.
WILLIAM WORDSWORTH

Martha wanted everything to be special. She changed the menu several times. Finally, she threw her shawl over her head and bustled off for the market.

Jesus was coming for supper. It would be the first time He had eaten with Mary and Martha since He raised Lazarus from the dead.

Meanwhile, Mary was outside, sitting in the garden. She, too, wondered how she could make tonight special for Jesus. An idea came to her, and she smiled, content with her decision. In anticipation, she bent over and picked a colorful bouquet of flowers for the table.

That evening, Martha placed the food on the table for her guests. The men savored the delicious aromas and ate heartily.

After the meal, Mary disappeared into her room. Her hands trembled as she picked up her precious alabaster jar of costly, spikenard ointment. It was worth a man's wages for an entire year, but at this moment her sacrifice meant nothing to her. With pleasure and anticipation she carried it to where Jesus reclined and knelt behind Him.

As she opened the jar, the air was immediately filled with luxurious fragrance from the ointment. Lovingly, Mary dipped her fingers into the jar and then, applying some of the balm, she anointed Jesus' feet, gently rubbing the ointment over them again and again.

When she finished her task, she loosened her hair covering and pulled her hair over her shoulder. With extreme tenderness, she wiped His feet, while tears of love spilled over them. When Jesus felt the tears, He turned His head and looked at her, smiling His approval. He accepted her act of love and devotion.

Mary lavishly gave her most costly possession to demonstrate her love for Jesus. Others objected. They felt she gave too much, that it would have better served if she had given it to the poor. Mary ignored their protests, keeping her eyes only on Jesus. Her heart was filled with her adoration for this One who had declared He was the resurrection and the life.

Is there some precious commodity in our lives which we can bring to Jesus to express our love to Him? We can't anoint His feet physically as Mary did, but we can lavish our love on Him by reaching out to His other children and demonstrating our love for them.

I'm going to check my alabaster jar of cherished possessions and decide which would be most fitting to present to Him. What do you have in your alabaster jar? — L.M.

"Mary therefore took a pound of very costly, genuine spikenard ointment, and anointed the feet of Jesus."
JOHN 12:3, NASB

Jesus,
teach me how to pour out my love for You extravagantly so
others will benefit from the fragrance of my act. Thank You.
Amen.

✳

Happily Ever After with Detours
In my end is my beginning.
Oh Lord my God, I have trusted in thee;
O Jesu my dearest one, now set me free.
MARY, QUEEN OF SCOTS

Many fairy tales end with the phrase, "They were married, and they lived happily ever after." Virtually every bride on her wedding day envisions this fairy tale ending in her life.

Esther's fairy tale came true when she was chosen queen of 127 provinces, stretching from India to Cush. At first, she hid her identity as a Jewess because she feared it might interfere with her fairy tale dream.

However, a crisis arose, and the lives of her people were at stake. Her uncle, Mordecai, told her to go into the king's presence and plead with him to save her people. Esther knew that anyone who approached the king in the inner court without being summoned would be put to death unless the king extended his golden scepter and spared the person's life. She knew her life was at stake.

Nevertheless, she agreed to go to King Xerxes. She said, "I will go to the king, even though it is against the law. And if I perish, I perish" (Esth. 4:16). She realized walking into the court palace might be the end.

However, what appeared to be the ending for Esther was really a new beginning. Perhaps God had brought her to that royal position specifically for that reason. King Xerxes granted Esther's petition, and she saved the lives of her people.

Unfortunately for many of us, our fairy tale can come to a sudden end with the death of a spouse or the death of a marriage. In my own life, the words spoken to me, "I care about you, but I don't want to be married to you anymore," symbolized the end of my fairy tale.

Now looking back on my divorce, I realize that what I thought was an ending was a new beginning for me, too. If I had remained in that marriage, I might not have developed the fulfilling career of writing, speaking, and editing that I now enjoy.

Nevertheless, it has been a long journey to wholeness. When I was first single, I assumed I would remarry immediately and begin a new fairy tale. I didn't feel whole without a mate. In time though, I realized I needed to complete the healing process. Before I could remarry and provide a man with the emotional support he needed, I must become whole myself.

I didn't know if, or when, I would remarry, but that ceased to be my focus. I reached a point where I was content where I was—where God had placed me at that particular point in time.

Today, I realize that I am healthier and happier in my new life than I ever was before.

To reach a sense of contentment, we must walk down the road God leads us. Living happily ever after often comes with detours. Like Esther, if we learn to depend on Him, we will not be afraid. — S.T.O.

> "And who knows but that you have come to royal position for such a time as this?"
> ESTHER 4:14

Dear God,
teach us not to be afraid when detours loom before us. Help us to realize that what seems like an ending may really be a new beginning. Amen.

*

His Heart of Love

God's fingers can touch nothing but to mold it into loveliness.
GEORGE MACDONALD

Wavelets lapped around my toes as I gingerly stepped along the rock-strewn shore of the Sea of Galilee. Dawn has always been the best part of the day for me. Rising early before my roommate did, I walked along the shore where Jesus had walked. Were my feet touching the same places His had?

Each morning as I strolled on the beach, I delighted with the sense of His presence. In my mind, I relived some of the scenes in Jesus' life which involved the Sea of Galilee.

The trip to Israel was a bonus I gave myself after my retirement from the engineering department where I worked over twenty-seven years. The journey to this historic land had so far brought joy and excitement. This morning, however, I felt oddly despondent. Tears came easily as loneliness surrounded me. Did my presence matter to anyone else in the group?

I walked slowly across the rocks and sand, pausing occasionally to gaze across the lake where Jesus had spent many hours with His disciples.

Glancing down, I saw something that made me stop—and gasp! A white rock was perched on top of other multicolored rocks as if it was waiting for someone to claim it. I did! I picked up the velvet-smooth stone and laid it in the palm of my hand.

Examining it, I could only wonder at the original shape of this piece of granite. Whatever the shape *had* been, the form of a heart now nestled in my hand. A heart-shaped rock!

How many years had that stone lain in the waters of the Sea of Galilee, gently caressed by the waves until it was shaped into its present form? Why hadn't someone else claimed this prize? It is because that rock wasn't meant for anyone else to claim. God meant it just for me—that very day.

I looked upward. "Father, thank You. This is so like You. How many years, or even centuries, have You allowed this stone to be formed into a heart? Did You fashion it with Your own fingers? Then, this very morning, when I desperately needed assurance of Your love, You tenderly placed it in my path. You have reminded me that no matter where I am, You are aware of me and how I feel. Thank You for loving me so much."

I held the rock in my hand for several moments, tracing its rounded shape with my fingers. I marveled at God's love.

Then, finally, I turned back toward the kibbutz, eager to rejoin my traveling companions. A new, exciting day beckoned, and I was ready for whatever might happen.

Our Heavenly Father cares for every one of us in the same way. His personal love and understanding are extended to each of us. We need to be aware of His signs.

As I tightly held that rock in my hand, confidence swelled within me. I knew that I, too, was held in a secure hand, a hand of love which would never let me go. — L.M.

"When my spirit was overwhelmed within me,
Thou didst know my path."
PSALM 142:3, NASB

Father,
help me to recognize those events in my life that You have
planned. Thank You for answering my needs and for making
me aware of Your love. In Jesus' name, Amen.

✳

A Thousand Ways

God has a thousand ways where I can see not one,
When all my means have reached their end,
Then His have just begun.
ESTHER GUYOT

On a hot summer day in July 1987, I stood in the Standard Publishing Booth on the floor of the Christian Booksellers Convention in Anaheim, California. As I shook hands with bookstore owners, I appeared confident on the outside with the excitement of having my first book, *Parables for Young Teens*, published. Yet, I hurt on the inside. My marriage of twenty-two years was about to end.

Questions unrelated to the convention excitement filled my mind. Could I make a living writing books? How could I help support my two college-age sons? How would I ever pick up the pieces of my life again?

Six months later, with heavy snow falling outside his parents' home in Boise, Idaho, Dick Osborn sat quietly in his room. Recently, a dating relationship had ended, and he felt empty. Reaching for his Bible, he read, "We toss the coin, but it is the Lord who controls the decision" (Prov. 16:33, TLB).

Normally he wasn't the type to give God an ultimatum, but this particular evening, he felt lonely and depressed thinking about Sandy. He reached in his pocket for a quarter and flipped it up in the air, saying, "Lord, if it comes down heads, I will marry Sandy. If it doesn't, I know that isn't Your will." The coin landed with the tails side up.

Glancing around the room, Dick's gaze fell on a *Lookout* magazine, lying upside down on the rug. On the back was an advertisement for *Parables for Young Teens*. Dick stared at the magazine and seeing my name pleaded, "Lord, who am I going to marry—Susan F. Titus?" Again, he flipped his coin up in the air, but this time it came down heads.

"Lord, you're not listening to me. I don't know anyone named Susan Titus. I don't even know what state she lives in. How could I possibly marry her?"

At the time, God seemed silent. However, on August 22, 1992, Dick and I were married.

It is exciting to think that when I was suffering from the emotional turmoil of a pending divorce, God already knew the course my life would take five years later. When I made the divorce decision, I hadn't worked full-time in twenty years. I didn't have a college degree, although I eventually obtained a bachelor of arts in religious studies and a master of arts in communications. I didn't have any idea how I would support myself, but God knew. When I stepped out in faith, He turned what had been an avocation into a full-time job.

Looking back over the past ten years, I never dreamed my life would take the path it has. When all I had to hold onto was a thread linking me to God, I learned to step out in faith and to take risks. If I had not been forced to earn a living, I never would have developed my current programs and ministries. After six years of being a single parent, I am now blessed with a supportive husband and a thriving business. — S.T.O.

"'I know the plans I have for you,'" declares the Lord,
"'plans to prosper you and not to harm you, plans to
give you hope and a future.'"
JEREMIAH 29:11

Dear Heavenly Father,
when I was suffering from my greatest emotional turmoil,
You were there. You had already determined the course of my
life. Thank You for caring so much. Amen.

✳